BEVERLY MASSACHUSETTS

QUARRY BOOKS

mixed media Doll Making

REDEFINING **THE DOLL** WITH **UPCYCLED MATERIALS**

LINDA AND OPIE O'BRIEN

First published in the United States of America by
Quarry Books, a member of
Quayside Publishing Group
100 Cummings Center
Suite 406-L
Beverly, Massachusetts 01915-6101
Telephone: (978) 282-9590
Fax: (978) 283-2742
www.quarrybooks.com
Visit www.Craftside.Typepad.com for a behind-the-scenes peek at our crafty world!

Originally under the following Library of Congress Cataloging-in-Publication Data

O'Brien, Linda, 1949-
  Who's your Dada? : redefining the doll through mixed media / Linda and Opie O'Brien.
    p. cm.
  ISBN-13: 978-1-59253-562-0
  ISBN-10: 1-59253-562-3
  1. Dollmaking. 2. Surrealism I. O'Brien, Opie, 1949- II. Title.
  TT175.O26 2009
  745.592'21—dc22

                                                                    2009014430

ISBN13: 978-1-59253-744-0
Digital edition published in 2011
eISBN: 978-1-61058-157-8

10 9 8 7 6 5 4 3 2 1

Cover Image: Dina A. Rossi
Photography: Dina A. Rossi with art direction by Linda and Opie O'Brien
Additional Photography: *Spoonfed*, all photos by Keith Lo Bue (pages 92–93 and 96–97); *Harleykin*, photo by Martin Fox Photography, courtesy of Lark Books (pages 128–129); *The Opera Singer*, photos by Denise Andersen Photography (page 135); and *The Doll That Went to Church*, photo by Marlene True (page 148)
Design: John Hall Design Group, www.johnhalldesign.com
Art Assistant: Ashley Hill

Printed in Singapore

to everyone who ever said:

i think i can

FROM LINDA O'BRIEN

Many people who have crossed my path over the years say I am an "old soul." Perhaps. What I know for certain is that I am drawn to the forgotten, forsaken, broken, and abandoned, be they people or objects, because left unattended or unacknowledged, their tiny spark of life can all too easily be extinguished. I like to fan the flames of creativity, because I believe there is an artist in each of us, whether we realize it or not, just waiting to come out and play.

Too often I hear people say that they are not creative, when more than likely all they really need is a place to start. I enjoy helping people discover their hidden potential and find their voice . . . someone once helped me, and it changed my life.

Being adopted, I always felt as if I didn't "belong." But artists are creative souls with a strong sense of community who share a special bond that goes beyond birthing and a biological gene pool. With every new artist, our community is enriched and we become part of something bigger than ourselves. A tribe . . . my tribe . . . and yours. Together we can make a difference and help restore our planet to its "green" place of whimsy, wonder, and fulfillment. Many of the materials are right here at our feet and our fingertips, items that have been thrown out, cast off, and discarded before their time, down but not quite out, just awaiting a new vision. Your vision. So if you haven't already discovered your inner artist, I hope this book will facilitate your journey.

I would also like to add that I am privileged to have co-authored this book with my husband, partner, artist, and soulmate Opie. This was truly a team effort. Even though the words you will read here are mine, Opie was the person responsible for the organizational end of it all, beginning with the projects, coordinating and preparing everything for the the photo shoots, and keeping it all under control . . . no easy feat. He is my rock and the other half of all that I am, and together we are Burnt Offerings.

Contents

Dadas in waiting

A collection of dolls from Thuringia, Germany, dug out from bombed doll factories

introdu(tion

Most of us played with dolls during our childhood, imagining and acting out story-lines, and for some of us, the experience helped prepare us for adulthood … or not!

Even today, Opie, who was more into action figures than dolls, still has his aunt's 1930s Shirley Temple doll, sitting in her place of honor as guardian and house-mother to all our dolls, recyclabots, and in-progress Dada dolls. As a child, I too had a special aunt and mentor who was a "travelin'" girl and worked for the government living in many countries. My Aunt Fran started my doll collection by sending me a doll from every country she visited. As a result, I became intrigued by the histories of the dolls, since many were neither traditional nor conventional, but each seemed to possess a sacred energy that touched me on a personal level and strongly influenced my artistic journey. We like to believe that the dolls we collect, our fetish dolls, minkisi, ritual, and burial dolls, directly precede the dolls we now create. Admittedly, our dolls have more whimsical personas, but hopefully they possess that same energy.

Living on the shores of Lake Erie affords us a unique opportunity to incorporate a limitless supply of found materials into our work and to reuse society's detritus, broken doll parts, vintage toys, building blocks, old photos, ephemera, and tin litho in new and exciting ways. Recycle, reduce, repurpose, reuse—these need to be more than just words. For artists, they should be a

Linda knew early on that Dadas would be a part of her future.

Dada Heads. These vintage Minerva and Juno heads are made of tin. The authors have been collecting them for years.

mantra for action. We live in a time when thinking green and being mindful of our planet and the materials we use and discard is essential. After making your first Dada, you'll discover a genuine joy that comes from giving new life to something destined for the scrap heap.

Over the past decade artists have pushed the limits of doll design, leaving us to wonder, "What is a doll?" We're really excited that the guest artists in this book have answered that very question. Our answer is in the evolution of our doll creations as we celebrate the unusual and absurd through the pairing of dissimilar objects, much like the artwork born of the Dada movement.

So . . . what is Dada, you ask?

Here's the condensed version, sans politics, and with a definite emphasis on the whimsical and absurd. Dada was a European cultural movement that involved visual arts, literature, theater, and graphic design. It began as a protest against World War I. The movement itself was very short lived, being essentially over by 1923, but it left a lasting legacy. The distintive work that came from this period included a virtual who's who of artists, including Picasso. The techniques and styles of Dadaism are so pervasive in modern art that it is not often given the recognition it deserves. In fact, without Dadaism, it's unlikely that surrealism and other modern art movements would have even occurred.

It's believed that the movement chose the name *Dada* by inserting a slip of paper into a French dictionary and choosing the word it landed on; *dada* happens to mean a hobbyhorse or child's toy. And in a "six-degrees of separation" kind of way, one of our contributing artists will share an interesting story that connects her piece to the ballet called *Parade*—first preformed by the Ballet Russes, and the collaboration between Erik Satie, Picasso, and Jean Cocteau. But back in the United States, somewhere around 1915, a body of artwork emerged that was driven by a sense of irony and humor, much like the dolls we're about to present in this book. We relate to this artistic perspective (perhaps because we too are transplanted New Yorkers, or maybe it was

something in the water, or perhaps Opie and I just have a really unusual sense of humor . . .).

In any event, while our love of dolls began at young ages, it is our love for each other that gave birth to our Who's Your Dada? series of whimsical, nontraditional, and often surreal dolls that we are privileged to share with you. This book is divided into three sections. The first section covers tools and a wide variety of techniques. The second section guides you through five step-by-step

projects, each featuring a different substrate so you'll learn how to work with wood, canvas, tin, books, and box constructions. You'll also find additional examples of our work and project variations from our students and artist friends. The final section goes quite beyond a simple gallery. It not only showcases the work of some of the most talented artists *ever* but also offers you a unique glimpse into their creative process, and shares their answer to the big question: How do *you* define a doll?

So let's get started.

Above: Christmas morning 1950. Opie, more obsessed with finding his little red wagon, didn't realize Dadas would be in his future. At right: A portion of the authors' wood block collection

OVER THE PAST DECADE ARTISTS HAVE PUSHED THE LIMITS OF DOLL DESIGN, LEAVING US TO WONDER, "WHAT IS A DOLL?

techniques and materials

Opie and I are avid recyclers who love to repurpose existing materials. So in keeping with our "path of least resistance" philosophy, you'll find that you already have many of the materials you'll need on hand and lots more that you can re-assign. A major perk of this is that your creations will be unique unto you—a bonus when working with found materials to begin with. Other materials can easily be found in your local craft store, secondhand store, or yard and garage sales. Think outside the box, or turn that box into a head or a body. As I always say, it's your party! We've also kept the techniques basic, doable, and limited to how we create our own work. You can keep it simple and still create interesting and outstanding art, so go through your stash, pull out some art supplies, and see what says Dada to you.

Linda's studio

tools

Your journey into Dada dollmaking begins with the gathering of a few simple tools and materials, many of which you probably already have since they are pretty basic. The rest are easy to find. Some projects require additional and more specific supplies, which are listed with the instructions for those particular projects.

BASIC TOOL KIT

- hammer
- pliers
- flat- and Phillips-head screwdrivers
- metal ruler with a cork backing
- awl or needle tool
- craft knife and scissors
- palette knife or craft stick
- sandpaper or sanding blocks in various grits of coarse, medium, and fine
- nylon and disposable foam paintbrushes
- container for water
- rags
- drill with various drill bits including: $1/16$", $3/32$", and $1/8$" (1.6, 2.4, and 3 mm)
- wire (we recommend 19-gauge dark annealed steel wire)
- assorted fasteners, small nails, micro-fasteners, screws, dowels, and screw eyes

OPTIONAL TOOLS
(but nice to have)

- heat gun (to speed up the drying process)
- mini-quilting iron and crayons (for special effects)
- toaster oven (for polymer clay)
- inexpensive clay or dental tools (for clay and Apoxie Sculpt)
- pop rivet gun, heavy tin snips, eyelets, and grommets
- files (optional for wood and metal)

BASIC PROJECT MATERIAL KIT

- acrylic paints and dye inks
- Apoxie Sculpt and/or polymer clay and/or paper clay
- found materials, doll parts, embellishments, and doodads
- five substrates: a wood block, a canvas frame, a tin can, an old book, or a wooden box

OPTIONAL MATERIALS
(but nice to have)

- crackle paints
- molding paste
- rubber stamps
- metallic foils
- wax
- flexible molds and mold-making kits
- glaze
- assorted fibers, waxed linen, and silk sari
- Lutradur, Rigid Wrap plaster gauze, cheesecloth, and paper

techniques

None of the techniques in this book are the only means to the end. They are simply the ones that work well for us and that we think you will have success with. The fact that most of them are interchangeable and can work with almost any substrate is also cost effective, requiring fewer materials, yet still providing you with a variety of options and the opportunity to make your own choices as you create.

Paints and inks become more than the sum of their parts.

COLORING WOOD

Unless you have a vintage toy block on hand that's perfectly sized and weather-worn by time, you'll most likely be starting with raw wood from a lumberyard or home improvement center. Pine is our wood of choice. Start with a piece of wood that is 2" (5.1 cm) thick × 4" (10.2 cm) wide by your desired length. For a nominal fee, the supplier will cut it to size for you, or if you're ambitious, you can cut it yourself with a hand or power saw. Once the wood is cut, sand it well, especially the edges, and wipe it clean. There are several ways to add color, but our two favorites, acrylic paints and inks, provide similar results.

Painting

Any acrylic paint you have on hand will work. If it's too thick, water it down to a consistency a bit heavier than a wash so it can be layered onto the surface, creating depth. Note that too much water can raise the grain on some raw wood. We usually use between three and five contrasting colors and start by applying light colors first, drying between layers, and often sanding off some of the color to give the wood a weather-worn look. We never rush this process and we work the wood until we're satisfied with the end result. If you take the time to build up your layers, it really shows. Our acrylic paints of choice, used for all the painted projects in this book, are Golden fluid acrylics, which require little or no diluting. I apply three contrasting color paints with a rag and rub the colors in, then add overall highlights with one or two additional colors. Opie prefers to paint with an inexpensive 1" (2.5 cm) flat, nylon brush.

Using Ink

Since any dye ink will work, you should use your favorite. We like Distress Ink from Ranger. You can apply these directly to the raw wood from the ink pad with a light touch, just as if you were using the direct-to-paper method. Wood is porous and takes ink beautifully. Select three to five contrasting colors and work from light colors to dark. It's especially important to dry between layers or you will muddy your ink pads by picking up wet inks. When we use this method, we start at one end of the wood substrate and run the pad all the way to the other end for the first one or two colors. (If you start in the middle, you'll form an unwanted line across the wood.) Then we apply any additional color with a makeup sponge (or similar tool) to add depth and highlights.

USING A HEAT GUN BETWEEN LAYERS WILL SPEED UP THE DRYING PROCESS. KEEP A RAG HANDY TO WIPE OFF ANY UNWANTED PAINT OR INK BEFORE IT HAS TIME TO SET.

DOS

ONCE YOU'VE FINISHED ADDING YOUR SPECIAL EFFECTS, YOU MAY WISH TO SEAL THE SURFACE WITH A MATTE MEDIUM. WAX IS THE EXCEPTION—IT'S A SEALER ITSELF.

GLAZES AND WASHES

Glazes are used to create extra depth. They are an alternative to fast-drying acrylics, allowing you to build up layers slowly and blend colors to your satisfaction. Glaze does not require additional sealer. If you like the effect, you can use glaze on the altered and collaged head *after* your head is completely transformed, totally dry, and either attached or ready to be attached to your body. Even after your head is permanently attached, you can still add more glaze or tissue (especially if you've filled in any uneven or open spaces with more Apoxie Sculpt). Our glaze of choice is Golden, which is basically a blend of Golden fluid acrylic colors and Golden acrylic glazing liquid, but you can also easily make your own glaze by adding acrylic paint to a commercially made glazing medium.

Washes are similar to glazes and are made by diluting acrylic paint with water. If you use washes, they'll need to be sealed. Before you make these decisions, all of your Dada's body elements should be laid out to give you an idea of your overall color scheme.

ADDING FINISHING TOUCHES AND SPECIAL EFFECTS TO SUBSTRATES AND SURFACES

For real pizzazz, the addition of crackle paints, molding paste, rubber stamp designs, metallic foils, and waxes provide the WOW factor. Almost

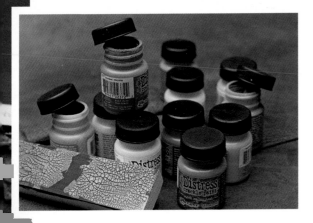

anything can be used to add layers of texture, like bubble wrap for imprinting a surface, and doilies and lace for stenciling. One look around your work area will likely offer up several choices.

Crackle Paint

Over the years we've tried a variety of crackle paints, but found them problematic or too labor intensive. Then we discovered Distress Crackle Paints, which are truly a one-step wonder. You can apply them right over an inked or painted surface or directly over gesso. They come in a variety of colors, and when you apply distress crackle paint over its corresponding distress ink, the effect is fantastic. The end result depends on how thickly or thinly you apply the crackle. The thicker the application, the larger the crackle effect and the longer it takes to dry. With a thin coat, the crackle effect is much smaller. Either way, if you act quickly, you can rubber stamp directly into it for a very cool effect, but don't forget to clean your stamps afterward.

Rubber Stamps

Rubber stamps can be used in a variety of applications. We stamp them into ink pads, acrylic paints, distress crackle paints, molding paste, clay, and Apoxie Sculpt. They come in many forms and sizes, from foam stamps to mounted or unmounted ones, and can be used to add text as well as texture. They are inexpensive, so you can build a collection of styles: alphabets, bold graphic stamps, or more detailed images. They clean up easily with either water or solvent.

Molding Paste

Molding paste, also called modeling paste, is suitable for use with almost any type of substrate whether it's painted, inked, or raw. Apply the paste with a palette knife straight from the jar, or you can even use an old credit card, craft stick, or your fingers. We particularly like its effect over dried crackle paint that has been stamped for additional texture. You can also apply the pastes through stencils for another interesting effect. Foam stamps and molding paste pair very well—regular rubber stamps work as long as they have a bold graphic. When the molding paste is dry, you can color over it with acrylic paint or inks.

Mounted, unmounted, metal, or foam, rubber stamps offer a wide range of applications.

Metal foils and crayones come in a variety of color choices.

Metallic Foils and Waxes

Foils and waxes add another layer of dimension, usually the final one, and are fun and easy to work with. Foils, which come in several colors, provide subtle metallic highlights that look especially cool applied over the raised surface of painted or inked molding paste. You only need a small amount for a big effect. Foils are applied with heat and a mini-quilting iron from the craft store. Make sure the shiny side of the foil is facing up when you touch the iron to it.

Wax is used in this book to accent and highlight. All you really need are a few children's crayons and a mini-quilting iron. Once the iron is hot, touch the tip of the crayon to the surface of the iron. This will melt the crayon and drip wax wherever you desire, eliminating the cost of a hot plate, special brushes, and expensive encaustic waxes. Sometimes less is more!

APOXIE SCULPT

Two-part epoxy putty, available under many different names, is not a new material. It's widely used by plumbers and other craftsmen. In 2007 we discovered Aves Apoxie Sculpt, an amazing, nontoxic, waterproof, two-part compound with puttylike consistency that you mix together when you're ready to use it. It's inexpensive, has a two to three-hour working time, no fumes, no shrinkage, and cures completely in 24 hours. Begin by blending, kneading, and twisting together equal amounts of each of the two-part compound for at least two minutes. The texture is similar to Silly Putty or Play-Doh. It is stickiest when first mixed and adheres anything to anything (although we do roughen up our surfaces a bit to ensure a really good bond). If you wait an hour or two for it to set, you can add details, and like clay, you can create faces and limbs either by hand or with a mold. Apoxie Sculpt can be seamlessly feathered before setup, or sanded, painted, drilled, carved, or otherwise tooled after setup, without chipping, cracking, or flaking. How cool is that! This product opens up a wealth of design possibilities. It comes in a variety of colors and has a shelf life of about a year. The one-pound size is a good choice if you are new to the product.

Throughout this book, Apoxie Sculpt is frequently used for attachment as well as in flexible molds. We leave the art of hand building faces and limbs for you to experiment with at your leisure once you've become comfortable with the product. A visit to its website provides in-depth tutorials about all of its products.

ALTERING AN EXISTING HEAD

Plastic doll heads are easy to come by at flea markets, secondhand and dollar stores, or on eBay, and are great fun to alter. The first thing you'll want to do is gather any objects you intend to incorporate into the head. You can either cut out portions of the head so you have holes to stick objects in, or you can affix objects with Apoxie Sculpt. If you wish to cut the head, use a sharp craft knife. Then, lightly sand the head

NEVER WASH
YOUR HANDS
OR CLEAN YOUR
TOOLS IN THE
SINK OR FLUSH
YOUR APOXIE
WATER, AS IT
CAN CLOG YOUR
DRAINS. KEEP
A CONTAINER
HANDY FOR
CLEANING YOUR
HANDS AND
TOOLS. SINCE
APOXIE SCULPT IS
NONTOXIC, YOU
CAN DISPOSE
OF THE WATER
OUTSIDE.

This Dada head
is awaiting her
transformation.

with medium-grit sandpaper or a sanding block
to give it some "tooth."

A technique for collaging the head and
connecting it to a body using dowels is featured in
the first project, page 32.

CREATING FACES AND LIMBS

While it's very exciting to find the perfect doll
part, hunting and gathering doesn't always
guarantee success. So, if you don't find *the* perfect
piece, why not make your own? This can seem
intimidating at first, but the promise of instant
gratification may win you over in the end (it
always does for me). And while you can definitely
hand build your own parts without a mold, it's a
process that requires personal vision, practice,
patience, and often some sort of an armature. So
for now, we'll focus on making body parts using
various molds.

Using Ready-Made Molds and Definition Tools

Molds can be purchased at craft stores or online. If the molds aren't exactly as you want them, customize or alter the features of the sculpting material once it is removed from the mold with simple clay tools, and by stretching, compressing, re-forming, and/or cutting off certain sections. Use inexpensive clay tools, available from the craft store, dental tools, a needle, toothpicks, a Popsicle stick, the point of a nail, or just about anything to move and manipulate the clay and create definition. If you're using Apoxie Sculpt, wait an hour or so after you remove it from the mold before you take the tools to it.

We favor flexible molds when using Apoxie Sculpt. First coat the mold with a mold release, such as a very thin coat of silicone lubricant, so you can remove the content without it sticking. You can also use petroleum jelly although it's a little heavier and a bit messier. You can make your own hard molds from polymer clay for use with polymer and paper clays; simply dust them with baby powder or cornstarch before filling them.

IF YOU'RE NOT HAPPY WITH YOUR MOLD IMPRESSION, YOU CAN PUT IT BACK IN THE MOLD, BUT DON'T REMIX THE APOXIE SCULPT BECAUSE IT'S COATED WITH LUBRICANT.

DADA DON'TS

Assorted Apoxie Sculpt and polymer clay heads

The Apoxie Sculpt Face

Mix Apoxie Sculpt *very* well for a minimum of two minutes. Make a ball with sort of a conical point for a nose and press it into your flexible mold with enough pressure to fill every crevice in the mold. Since the mold is flexible, you can even apply pressure from the other side of the mold. Carefully remove the material as soon as possible.

Place the Apoxie Sculpt face immediately on its background substrate for the best adhesion and so you can embed objects immediately. After it sets up for an hour, add definition with the tools we mentioned earlier, being careful not to pull it off its substrate. Once it's dry, you can highlight it with paints or metallic rub-ons, paint the face completely, or even drill through it (a great feature should you decide after the fact to add last-minute embellishments or discover too late that you forgot to embed something). The possibilities are wide open and it's never too late to make adjustments.

The Polymer Clay Face

Polymer clay is a nontoxic, oven-baked clay and a very popular choice among artists. It requires baking and we recommend a toaster oven dedicated to crafts—not one you use for food. For optimal success, follow the manufacturer's instructions because baking temperatures and times vary with each brand. Most clays require some conditioning. If only a little conditioning is required, you can knead and warm up the clay with your hands. If more is required, you might need to run the clay through a pasta machine several times. This also strengthens the clay. Once your clay is ready, dust your mold. Roll your clay into a ball, then flatten it slightly to the shape of the mold, press it in, then pop it out. You can alter the clay and add definition prior to baking by using the tools previously mentioned. You can also color enhance the clay prior to baking it with mica or pigment powders, chalks, eye shadow, Pearl-Ex, and even acrylic paints, or you can add color after it's been baked and cooled with everything from acrylics to watercolors to heat-set artist oils. You can use antiquing techniques to bring out highlights by painting the face with a darker acrylic paint such as burnt umber, brown, or black and then wiping it off with a rag. Repeat the process until you're happy with the results or just scrub it clean and simply start again. We often add metallic finishes to our pieces. Some paints and finishes may require a sealer.

The Paper Clay Face

Paper clay is an air-drying modeling clay that is ready to use straight from the package. Like polymer clay, you can use it with a mold. While we've personally never had much success with paper clay, its popularity merits inclusion. Two of our contributing artists, Linda Horn and Shain Erin, share their very different techniques for working with it on pages 124 and 106 respectively. Keep the paper clay refrigerated in a plastic bag to increase its shelf life. Recommended paper clays are from the company Creative Paperclay, which offers the following choices:

◆ **ORIGINAL PAPERCLAY:** a clay you can sculpt, shape, mold, or add color to while moist, and/or add color with either paint or pigment after it air-dries.

◆ **DELIGHT:** a newer clay that is light, soft, and easy to work with. The package says it won't stick to your fingers and picks up details easily.

◆ **DIAMOND:** the premium brand from Japan (the print on the package is in Japanese) is whiter in color and dries harder providing an extra-durable product. Many doll artists use it for building armatures or to give added strength to very small thin pieces such as fingers. This clay is a little harder to sand after it is dry.

DADA DON'Ts

NEVER THROW AWAY LEFTOVER APOXIE SCULPT. YOU CAN USE IT TO CREATE LITTLE DOODADS SUCH AS BEADS, RUBBER-STAMPED CHARMS, OR FACES AND INCORPORATE THEM INTO OTHER PROJECTS.

Making Your Own Polymer Clay Molds

Making your own molds can be a rewarding experience because you have the option to create them from objects that have special meaning to you. While we were in France, one of our students was really into making custom molds, so we carried conditioned clay with us wherever we went, and we made impressions from some very unique statuary. Now, whenever we use these molds, we think about the south of France and the memories we made there—Maureen's laughter and mischievious late-night humor—and our dolls feel that much more special.

We create our molds using both polymer clay and flexible mold-making kits.

To make a mold from polymer clay, start with well-conditioned clay and press it firmly over the surface you want to make an impression of, getting the clay into every nook and cranny. Remove the clay from the substrate and bake it according to the package directions. In addition to creating faces, you can use this method to create limbs. It bears repeating that this kind of mold should only be used with polymer and paper clay. Apoxie Sculpt will stick to the surface.

Using a Mold-Making Kit

To make a flexible mold, start with a two-part mold-making kit from the craft store. There are several brands and all of them work pretty much the same way. Start with two equal parts of the mold-making putties and knead them together, mixing them well. Then press your dimensional object into it. Once the material hardens, peel off the mold. Most molds cure in less than ten minutes, creating a mold that can be reused again and again. You can use these types of molds with Apoxie Sculpt, polymer clay, or air-dry clay.

The Instant Gratification Limb

It's always nice to have a backup plan, whatever the situation, so here's a great way to make a lightweight limb. Sometimes the substrate isn't sturdy enough to support a heavy limb, like in

Polymer clay molds made by the authors during a workshop in France

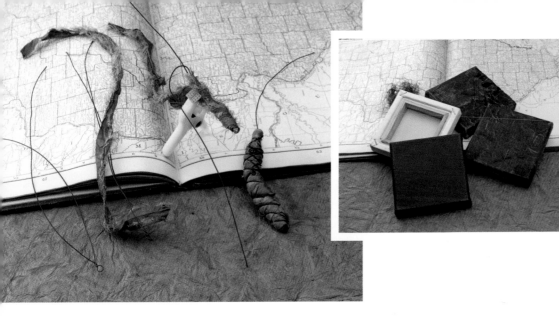

NEVER JUDGE
A MOLD BY
ITS OUTWARD
APPEARANCE, IT'S
WHAT'S INSIDE
THAT COUNTS!
YOU WOULD
NEVER KNOW
FROM LOOKING
AT A PAIR OF OUR
TUBE-SHAPED
FLEXIBLE MOLDS
THAT THEY
ACTUALLY MAKE
A REALLY COOL
PAIR OF DOLL
LEGS. IN FACT,
THEY ARE USED
IN LINDA'S BOX-
CONSTRUCTION
VARIATION
PROJECT, PAGE 91.

the box-construction Dada diary project (page 80). The box we selected for the body was perfect for the piece, although the wood itself was a bit thin. Because of this, almost all of the attachment techniques could split the wood, leaving wire as the most logical connection choice. This instant gratification limb, which is as light as a feather, was the perfect solution since we wanted to avoid anything too weight bearing.

The technique requires 19- or 20-gauge wire and almost any kind of fabric cut or torn into long thin strips for wrapping. Strips of silk sari are a great choice, but any ribbon, waxed linen, embroidery floss, or similar material is fine. If you like it and it wraps around the wire, then you can use it.

Begin with wire about 2' (61 cm) long. The length of the wire depends on the overall size of the doll and whether you are making arms or legs, since less wire is required for arms and more for legs. With a little practice, you'll determine the exact amount of wire required. Fold the wire in half and form a loop; twist the wire twice at the loop, and extend both wire ends from the loop. Insert your fabric strip between the two lengths of wire and wrap it around the wire, until you've achieved the desired length. Then take one of the wire lengths and wrap it around the fabric strip back down toward the loop, trapping and securing the fabric at the same time. The end result is very similar to a wire-wrapped fabric bead and provides both a unique look and a

perfect solution when you're dealing with thinner substrates. Trim the remaining end of the wire and insert it into a hole that you've drilled in the box for the arms and/or legs and connect it with a decorative spiral wrap (page 58), a loop, or basically any wire wrap that appeals to you.

COLLAGING CANVAS SUBSTRATES

Canvas substrates are perfect for collaging. Start by applying any color gesso to the canvas, covering both sides completely. (Gesso is a product used like paint primer to prepare a surface for painting or other surface design.) Then, use gel medium or white glue to apply thin tissuelike papers over both sides of the substrate. Mulberry paper, tissue paper, and rusting paper (see page 24) are excellent collage materials. Collaging with fabric scraps works equally well. Once it's collaged, add additional coats of white glue or gel medium to give it a really durable finish. If you want to add a bit of pizzazz prior to sealing it, incorporate some of the special effects techniques or add a few subtle hairlike fibers into it, such as Angelina, recycled silk, or silk thrums.

ONCE YOU'VE
FINISHED
RUSTING, KEEP
THE MUSLIN
FABRIC THAT YOU
COVERED THE
STEEL WITH TO
INCORPORATE
INTO OTHER
PROJECTS,
BECAUSE IT
NOW HAS A
BEAUTIFULLY
RUSTED,
PATINATED
FINISH.

RUSTING PAPER AND METAL

Whether it's metal or paper, we really love rust. There are kits, such as Sophisticated Finishes from Modern Options, that will chemically rust or antique practically any surface; however, rusting metal and paper is something you can do quite easily with a few household ingredients.

We like to rust our steel naturally by keeping it outside and turning it occasionally until we're happy with the results. Sometimes we mist it with a mixture of equal parts water and white vinegar to speed up the process. But if leaving steel outside of your home isn't an option, you can rust nongalvanized steel indoors. You'll need a large plastic garbage bag, a water misting bottle filled with equal parts water and vinegar, a piece of muslin fabric large enough to cover the steel, cold rolled steel (see Resources, page 158), and a large tray. Place the steel on the tray and mist it completely with the water and vinegar mixture. Cover the steel with the muslin and mist the muslin. Place the tray inside the garbage bag and close it with a twist tie; weight it down with a brick or heavy books. Open the bag and mist the muslin every so often until you like the color of the steel—the longer you leave the steel in the bag, the darker the rust becomes.

Use the rusted steel to make rust paper. There are several types of paper that can be rusted, but avoid those such as mulberry papers that contain a lot of fiber. Our favorite paper to rust is pattern tissue.

Simply place the paper right on top of the rusted steel and mist it with water. Let it dry and peel it off once the paper has rusted to your satisfaction.

THE FOUND OBJECT HEAD

A head can be made from almost anything you find interesting, but its actual success comes from you being able to seamlessly attach it to the body. Forethought is the key to success, so once you've gathered your components together, think about how you're going to attach them all *before* you begin. Like a well-stocked pantry, you should have on hand assorted small nails, mini- and micro-fasteners, nuts, screws and bolts, along with a drill, some drill bits, and Apoxie Sculpt.

TINKERING WITH TIN

We've been working with tin for more than ten years thanks to the one and only "tin-man" Bobby Hansson, a.k.a. Professor Bobo, author of *The Fine Art of the Tin Can* (Lark Books, revised edition 2005). We've made lots of dolls and sculpture using both intact and deconstructed tin. Since this book wouldn't be complete without a Tin Can Dada, here are some things to keep in mind when working with tin.

Deconstructing a tin can requires a can opener, a rubber mallet, heavy-duty tin snips (also called aviation snips) and detail-cutting tin shears. Remove

The authors have thousands of tin cans on hand.

the top and bottom with the can opener, and cut the rim and side seam with tin snips, so you can flatten the tin with a mallet. Once the tin is deconstructed, put your heavy-duty tin snips away and switch to detail-cutting tin shears, which are much lighter than tin snips. They allow you to shape curves and make precision cuts. Detail shears are also great for cutting all nonferrous metals, such as copper, sterling, nickel, and brass up to 22 gauge or .025" like butter. Thicker brass, which is the hardest of these metals, may require the heavier duty tin snips.

The key to cutting safely and accurately is to turn your metal into the blade as you're cutting, cut slowly in a counterclockwise motion, take small, baby cuts, and *never* let your blades meet. Careful cutting eliminates the need to file the edges, although if you happen to get a rough edge, you can almost always hammer it out with a mallet on a steel block. If you must file, only file in one direction—away from you.

The most common and popular attachments for tin are wire, pop rivets, eyelets, and grommets.

CREATING A DADA DIARY

This is a very unusual book because it features materials not often associated with traditional bookmaking. Gather your materials. We used Lutradur, which is a 100 percent polyester spun bond (a nonwoven translucent web material), similar to interfacing, for the cover substrate, Rigid Wrap, cheesecloth, waxed linen, watercolor paper, wallpaper, and specialty and amate papers. An interesting variation using screen, Paper Perfect, and inclusions follows. You can make your diary any size; simply measure the box or body it will be part of. The measurements don't need to be exact since there will be design variables—you might want to make a paper mock-up with scrap papers first.

The Covers

Cut a piece of Lutradur slightly smaller than the desired height and twice the width of the diary. For example, the space in our Dada diary box project is 5½" × 4½" (14 × 11.4 cm), so we cut the Latrudur 5¼" × 8¾" (13.3 × 22.2 cm). Fold the Lutradur in half, but don't cut it.

Next, cut two pieces of Rigid Wrap, also known as plaster cloth, the same size as the Lutradur. Cut them in half and briefly dip one in water. Working on one side at a time, place the wet Rigid Wrap over the Lutradur and let it dry. When that side is dry, repeat the process on the other sides.

Once the Rigid Wrap has completely dried on both sides of the Lutradur, rough-cut a piece of cotton cheesecloth larger than the open piece of Lutradur (the cheesecloth can be trimmed after it has dried, although a ragged edge has a nice look as well). Manipulate the size of the cheesecloth by stretching and pulling it. Coat the Rigid Wrap with gel medium or white glue and *loosely* lay the cheesecloth over the Rigid Wrap so you can bend the diary in half later without difficulty. Once the cheesecloth is dry, color it with distress inks or dry-brush it with acrylic paints. Do *not* rewet it.

Diary Variations

You can substitute screen (available in hardware or home improvement stores) instead of Lutradur for your cover, along with Paper Perfect, an interesting product from DecoArt, instead of cheesecloth. Paper Perfect is a paint that consists of actual paper fibers, allowing you to create handmade paper by spreading it direct from the jar (stir it well first) onto your substrate with a palette knife or a fan brush. Use it alone or

DOS
DADA

WHEN MAKING A DIARY COVER, FIRST DO ONE SIDE AND LET IT DRY COMPLETELY BEFORE APPLYING THE RIGID WRAP TO THE OTHER SIDE OR YOUR SUBSTRATE MIGHT WARP.

Paper Perfect and hardware store screen provide a unique cover variation.

mix it with fibers, glitter, flowers, and any other inclusions suitable for making handmade paper. You can even make entire custom sheets of paper by spreading Paper Perfect on a vinyl surface such as plastic sheet protectors or on a craft sheet and peeling it off after it has completely dried. It's nontoxic and comes in a variety of colors.

The Pages

Make the pages from 140 lb. watercolor paper, wallpaper, or specialty papers—alone or in combination. We favor Mexican bark paper, also known as amate paper, but it's difficult to find in the United States and can be pricey. Cut two pieces a tiny bit smaller than the covers and fold them in half. Since the depth of our box/body is only ¾" (1.9 cm), we folded our covers and pages in half to accommodate four pages, but if you have more depth, instead of folding your book exactly in half, make three folds, allowing for a deeper spine and more pages.

Binding

Binding the diary is the last step and a simple pamphlet stitch works great with this particular book. Hold the pages together and poke three holes with an awl: a center hole and holes about 1" (2.5 cm) from the top and 1" (2.5 cm) from the bottom. Bind the book with wax linen, starting with a piece about three times longer than the height of the book (we prefer to have more than we need, rather than less).

Begin on the outside of the spine and bring the thread into the center hole, leaving about an 8" (20.3 cm) tail. Take the thread back out either the top or bottom hole and then come back in the remaining hole. Exit out the center hole and when you do, you'll see a long stitch on the spine and two end tails staggered on either side of the long stitch. Tie and knot over the long stitch. Because this book needs to fit into the box/body, we trimmed the tail instead of embellishing it.

Finishing

Once the book is bound, embellish it any way you like—sew into it, collage over it, use wax crayons, inks, paints, transfers, wax, and any of the techniques covered in the wood substrate section. And, if you preplanned your cover sizes to include a beaded border, bead around the edges for another really cool effect. The most important thing to remember is that there are no hard and fast rules regarding size and design of the pages. It is a good idea to plan the pages in advance, but even after the diary is finished, if the pages don't quite fit, you can always adjust them by trimming or adding a border.

THE FINE ART OF ATTACHMENT

Attachment is about making connections, or joins. Different attachment techniques are covered individually in each project so you can see how, where, and when they are used, and why one attachment may be preferred over another.

There are only two kinds of joins, hot and cold. Basically, hot joins require heat from a torch, soldering iron, or kiln, and cold joins require no heat at all. Wire, nails, brads, screws, miniature lag screws, nuts, bolts and washers, micro-fasteners, brad fasteners, rivets, eyelets/grommets, dowels, and Apoxie Sculpt are examples of the cold joins used in this book. Most of the attachment materials can be found in your local hardware store, or in the supply/resource list in the back of the book (page 158). Here's a bit more about them.

◆ **WIRE:** we prefer 19-gauge dark annealed steel wire or 20-gauge copper.

◆ **NAILS:** escutcheon pins are either brass or brass-plated nails; a good overall size is ½" (1.3 cm) × 18 gauge.

◆ **BRADS:** smaller than nails, ½" (1.3 cm) × 20 gauge.

◆ **SCREWS:** steel drywall screws in 6" × ⅞₆" × 20 gauge size (15.2 cm × 1.1 cm × 20 gauge).

◆ **SCREW EYES:** small screws with eyelets at one end. The screw part screws into the substrate and usually wire goes through the eyelet part to form the attachment.

◆ **MINIATURE FASTENERS:** lag screws and their matching nutdrivers (a special tool that's used with them), machine screws, nuts, washers, and nails can be found in many hobby shops or at either micromark.com or reactivemetals.com.

◆ **MICRO-FASTENERS:** used to connect the head

to the frame in the Dos Dada project; they can be found at microfasteners.com.

◆ **BRASS FASTENERS:** used to connect the head to the box in the Dada Diary Project; they can be found at office-supplies.us.com.

◆ **POP RIVETS:** small-headed pins with an expandable shank for joining layers of light-gauge metal. The rivet assembly is inserted into a hole drilled through the parts to be joined and a pop rivet gun is used to draw the mandrel into the rivet. This expands the end of the rivet and then the mandrel snaps off. They come in copper, steel, stainless, nylon, and more, but the ⅛" (3 mm) aluminum ones are easiest to work with. We often use them with Tin Can Dadas.

◆ **EYELETS:** used with an eyelet setter, a setting block, and a hammer. Available in ¹⁄₁₆" (1.6 mm),

⅛" (3 mm), ¼" (6 mm), and 3⁄16" (4.8 mm) sizes from most craft stores, online, and at coffeebreakdesign.com.

◆ **GROMMETS:** basically oversized eyelets, only a bit more industrial and sturdier and can often be found in the fabric section of many craft stores. They often come with a heavier setting tool, which works the same as an eyelet setting tool, except it's bigger.

◆ **DOWELS:** wood rods that come in several diameters and lengths. We use them in constructing everything from dolls to assemblages, as either connections or armatures, but especially to connect a head to a body.

◆ **APOXIE SCULPT:** a self-hardening two-part synthetic clay that combines the features and benefits of clay with those of epoxies. It's UV resistant, waterproof, weatherproof, drillable, and incredibly durable. It comes in several colors, although it's also paintable, and we use it as an attachment method, as well as for creating molded faces and limbs. You can order it direct from avesstudio.com, with many of its sister products that work in similar ways, such as Apoxie Clay, Fixit Sculpt, or Aves ClayShay, a powder product that feels like clay but sets like mache. Their website has lots of information, user galleries, and more.

Projects and Variations

Now that you are familiar with many cool techniques, it's time to "hit the ground running" and use them. Think of the technique section as an old friend that you can revisit often. To assist you in creating your own Dadas and to provide you with the richest experience possible, we've selected five different substrates that utilize a variety of techniques and more important, a variety of attachments, so you'll always have choices and options. In step-by-step fashion, you'll see the fundamentals of working with each type of structure. After each project, we've included several variation projects from our students. Each student started with the same basic core materials and instructions, but added his or her own found materials and personal objects, just as you will with your dolls. Many of our students had never made a doll or worked with any of these materials. Yes, their dolls are amazing and yours will be too.

There are even a few variations that we've created, as well as a couple from some of the Gallery of Odd Dolls and Dadas artists whose particular piece was a perfect example for a certain project category. It's important to remember that there are no hard and fast rules about which attachment techniques to use. The choice will *always* depend on the objects you choose to incorporate. It's likely that your objects will differ from ours. Not a problem; mix it up and just have fun with it.

As a special bonus, this section will conclude with a visual progression of artist Keith Lo Bue's Odd Doll. So gather your found materials, cool doodads, and (dare we say) *junque*, and let's create some Dadas.

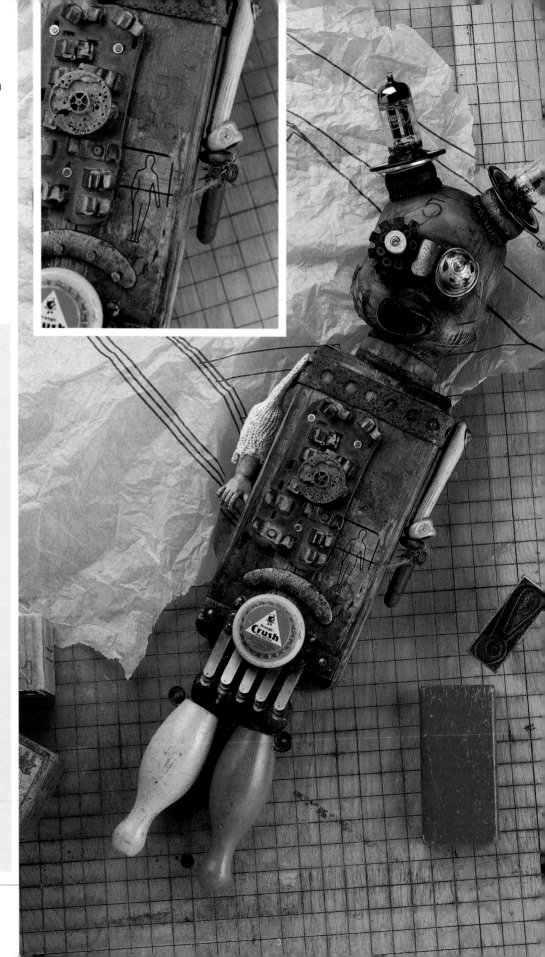

I've Got the Music in Me. Linda constructed this arm with objects found on the shores of Lake Erie and attached it with a wire connection.

MATERIALS

- ◆ basic tool kit (page 13)
- ◆ basic project material kit (page 13)
- ◆ hard plastic doll head (ours came from eBay)
- ◆ tissue paper (we used pattern tissue)
- ◆ favorite adhesive or white glue
- ◆ wood substrate, cut to approximately 2" × 4" × 6" to 8" (5.1 × 10.2 × 15.2 to 20.3 cm) (actual size depends on head size)
- ◆ found objects, doodads, doll parts to incorporate into the head, body, and limbs
- ◆ Apoxie Sculpt
- ◆ additional surface treatment materials (optional)
- ◆ armature supports (optional)
- ◆ glaze (optional)
- ◆ wire (19-gauge dark annealed steel wire)
- ◆ small nails (for the arms) and two screw eyes (for the legs)
- ◆ two wood dowels, one ¼" (6 mm) smaller in diameter, each about 6" (15.2 cm) long (can be trimmed to exact size later) *Note: one dowel should fit snugly into the opening of the neck of the doll head, the length running from the top of the head to the inside of the neck opening; the other dowel should be approximately ¼" (6 mm) smaller in diameter.*
- ◆ ³⁄₁₆" (4.8 mm)-wide dowel (if you're using a dowel as an armature support)

i've got the music in me

The core substrate for this Dada doll is a wood block. In addition to Apoxie Sculpt, wire, nails, and screw eyes, this doll features the dowel within a dowel attachment. Adapt your embellishments and found materials as desired.

I've Got the Music in Me. Opie altered an existing doll head and embellished it with various found materials. The tubes on top were from his vintage Fender Twin amplifier that he deconstructed after it "gave up the ghost," and they sit inside tin wheels from an advertising truck and vintage game pieces.

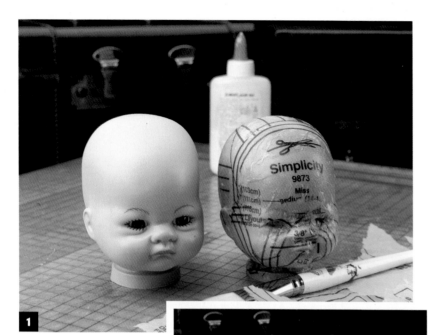

STEP 1 Alter the Head
Lightly sand the head with medium-grit sandpaper or a sanding block to give it some tooth. If you plan to insert items into the head (like into an eye socket), cut those areas out of the head with a craft knife. Cover the head with a collage of thin tissue paper and your favorite adhesive (Opie prefers plain old white glue; while I prefer medium). Set the head aside to dry.

STEP 2 Add Supports
Add or insert additional supports and/or armatures, such as a 3/16" (4.8 mm) dowel or heavy gauge wire into the head. You can drill right through the head to do this, but be careful to leave room for the center dowel attachment, which will run straight up through the neck to the top of the head. Gather the found objects you're going to incorporate into the head and insert any of them into the holes.

STEP 3 Finish the Head
Mix the Apoxie Sculpt components for at least two minutes (page 18). The Apoxie Sculpt is stickiest right after mixing, so use it immediately to attach or embed your objects on or into the head. Set the head aside for an hour or two, and then carefully add definition with any of the tools mentioned previously (page 20). Set the head aside again until it is completely dry.

STEP 4 Color the Wood
Sand and wipe clean your wood substrate and color it with paints or inks (page 15). As you can see in the photograph, the paints and inks produce very similar results. The wood on the left is painted; the one on the right is inked. For this doll, we used the inked substrate, and after it dried we added some finishing touches with crackle paint, rubber stamps, and wax (pages 16–17).

STEP 5 Creating the Dowel Attachment
The attachment for this head uses a dowel within a dowel, and since a picture is worth a thousand words, these photographs say it all.

Using a 1/4" (6 mm) drill bit, drill a hole, approximately 1" (2.5 cm) deep, into the center of

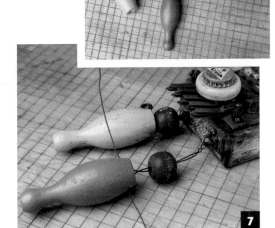

the top of the wood block body and the middle of the larger dowel. You can attach the dowels now, or if it's easier you can wait until after the rest of the body is complete. Simply insert the ¼" (6 mm) dowel into the holes in both the wood block and the larger dowel. You'll eventually place the finished Dada head over the dowel.

STEP 6 Gather Your Elements

Gather all the remaining found objects and embellishments for the body, plus nails, wire, and screw eyes for the attachments. This should give you a pretty good idea of your Dada's color composition, so when your head has totally dried, you can glaze it if you wish.

STEP 7 Attach and Secure the Limbs

Secure your surface embellishments to the body with a combination of nails, screws, and Apoxie Sculpt, and then set it aside to dry.

The arms on this Dada are simply nailed into the body with small escutcheon pins. One arm is a rescued doll arm, and the other is made from reclaimed wood found on the lakeshore. The "hand" is wired to the long wooden "arm" and then nailed to the substrate.

Two vintage children's bowling pins and two old, weathered beads make the legs. To attach them, or similar objects, drill a ¼" (6 mm) hole in the center of the wide bottom of the bowling pins, and a smaller ³⁄₃₂" (2.4 mm) hole on each side, at a slight angle so they meet at the center hole, for easier wire insertion.

Drill two tiny ¹⁄₁₆" (1.6 mm) pilot holes in the lower edge of the body so it's easier to attach the

two screw eyes. Once the screw eyes are in, cut two 18" (45.7 cm) lengths of wire (cut a length longer than you think you need). Run one of the wires halfway through a screw eye, fold it in half, and twist it once below the screw eye. Insert both wire ends through a bead and then into the center hole of the bowling pin, bringing each end of the wire out one of the side holes. Use flat-nosed pliers to shape the visible wire on each side of the leg into a spiral. Repeat for the remaining leg.

To permanently attach the head to the body, place a layer of Apoxie Sculpt around the underneath rim of the neck. Place the head over the larger dowel, pushing it all the way down to the substrate block, turning it a little, lifting it back off just a tiny bit and then pushing it right back on again. This movement creates tack. Allow the compound to fully cure overnight.

DOS

KEEP A RAG AND WATER CONTAINER NEARBY TO RINSE OFF YOUR FINGERS AND TOOLS.

VARIATIONS

Each of these dolls was created by our students in a one-day workshop. Everyone was given the same basic supplies: a plastic doll head, dowels for the head attachment, and a precut and sanded pine wood block for the body. We supplied paints and inks, the fasteners, and also brought a box of found materials that we collected from the lake. Students were asked to bring a few basic tools and their own special objects to incorporate. Everyone received the same instructions as are on pages 32–35 for this project.

Lauren Ohlgren

About the Artist

Lauren's life goal is to inspire others to create. She teaches *Travel Journal* classes. In 2005, she founded The She Project, which attracts more than 150 local women participants annually. Her book, *The She Project: How She Inspired a Community,* won the Independent Publisher Book Award and the Nautilus Book award in 2008. In her studio, Lauren's focus is encaustic, a medium that combines hot wax, resin, and pigment. With her first love being her ability to share and teach creativity, Lauren renews her energy by having frequent torrid affairs with different media through experimentation or by attending workshops.

> I think a doll is defined by emotions rather than characteristics. This means that a doll to one person may simply be an object to another. I also think that the emotions evoked are due to a common thread that the viewer shares with the doll—some human trait that could be real, imaginary, or symbolic.

PROCESS **Untitled**

Lauren collaged the head with pattern tissue and diluted glue. She attached found metal objects with Apoxie Sculpt, and after an hour, carved designs into it. Lauren tinted everything with paints for a cohesive look and distressed the block body using ink pads and rubbing in the color with her fingers. She cut a section from a beer can for the backside, along with a found hinge and metal tag and attached weather-worn scrap metal by hammering tacks into the existing holes. This feature became Lauren's favorite part of the doll, since it allowed her to appreciate and see trash in a new and different light. Lastly, she made arms and legs from various metal pieces, bisque doll parts, and dice and attached them with fragments of chain, washers, and wire.

Untitled. Lauren Ohlgren collaged an existing head, built it up, and attached her elements using Apoxie Sculpt.

Suzanne Sattler

About the Artist

Sue is an interior designer by profession and has always loved fabric and color, so when she became interested in dollmaking, it was no surprise that she would find ways to incorporate her favorite things. After taking several workshops with Opie and me, her palette broadened to include metal, wood, and found objects, and she has gained a clearer understanding of the art of attachment. Her pieces feature an interesting selection of objects that are full of whimsy and always "so Sue" and I'm privileged that over the years, we have become very close friends.

> "To me a doll is an artful expression of feelings, moods, and movement. This art form allows me to combine all the elements I love—fabrics, beads, and found materials to best express my way of creating."

PROCESS Lovely Lucille

Sue opted to create her head with Super Sculpey, her favorite of all polymer clays. She only uses Apoxie Sculpt for attachment purposes. Prior to baking, she put holes in the ears, as well as the top of the head, so she could later secure them with wire. She also made a larger hole at the bottom to attach the neck to the body. Using acrylics, the artist painted the head and hair and added copper wire, beads, and found objects to embellish the head, finishing with one found earring and another she picked up in her travels during our workshop in France. She painted the body with acrylics, rubbed them off in various spots, and then collaged with assorted papers. Sue drilled a hole at the top to attach the head. She used metal lamp parts as breasts and attached them with Apoxie Sculpt. She turned typewriter parts, beads, shoe taps, and iron lamp samples into arms and the legs, and wired everything to screw eyes.

Lovely Lucille. Suzanne Sattler took her doll in a new direction by creating a head from clay instead of altering an existing one.

Shelley d Schorsch

About the Artist

Shelley's fine arts education was in watercolor and printmaking, mediums that never seemed to fulfill her artistic craving and seemed to stunt her abilities. A terrific husband and five wonderful kids encouraged her to find her perfect creative outlet. During that journey, Shelley has worn many hats from interior designer to senior vice president of a public corporation. Currently she loves to crazy quilt and is an amateur ballroom dancer. She considers herself a mostly self-taught assemblage and collage artist and for the first time in her life that title sits well with her. Shelley told us that she appreciates that we helped her finally get over her fear of "Starting."

> Dolls have always been representational to me. As a child, a doll was my baby or sibling and became players in my imaginary games. I had a large 'walking' doll and a bunch of stuffed animals that did my bidding without back talk and played a huge role in my childhood. By the time I was fourteen, they were put aside as 'boys' and being a teenager became more important, *but* in my bedroom, these old friends still had a welcome place that I would return to in times of stress or sadness. Dolls are now back my life and still representational; the difference is that they now represent feelings, ideas, thoughts, or even a whim or two. Not having a particular style, I use whatever I have on hand and feel that the creation often comes from a part of me that I don't even know exists.

PROCESS Till Death Do Us Part

After Shelley received her component parts, she started auditioning different pieces from her bottomless stash of personal objects. When she had a general idea of what the doll would look like, she painted the wood block body with fluid acrylics to give the body an aged look. She then sanded the edges and rubbed distress inks on and off with a paper towel until she was satisfied with the color. Using Apoxie Sculpt for the first time (which she decided she loved), Shelley bonded her unique choice of pieces to the head and body and then collaged sheet music to the head, which softened it and added just the right touch. She also attached a tin nicho containing a mini assemblage to the body and continued applying Apoxie Sculpt to the head until she achieved a unified look. When the Apoxie Sculpt was dry she painted the head with acrylic washes, attached the limbs with wire, and used more Apoxie Sculpt to attach the little car and girl figure to the shoulder piece. Lastly, she glued the game board pieces to the front and back of the wood body base, made a few final color adjustments and her doll was complete.

> "IF IT'S NOT ONE THING, IT'S YOUR MOTHER."
> —ANITA RENFRO

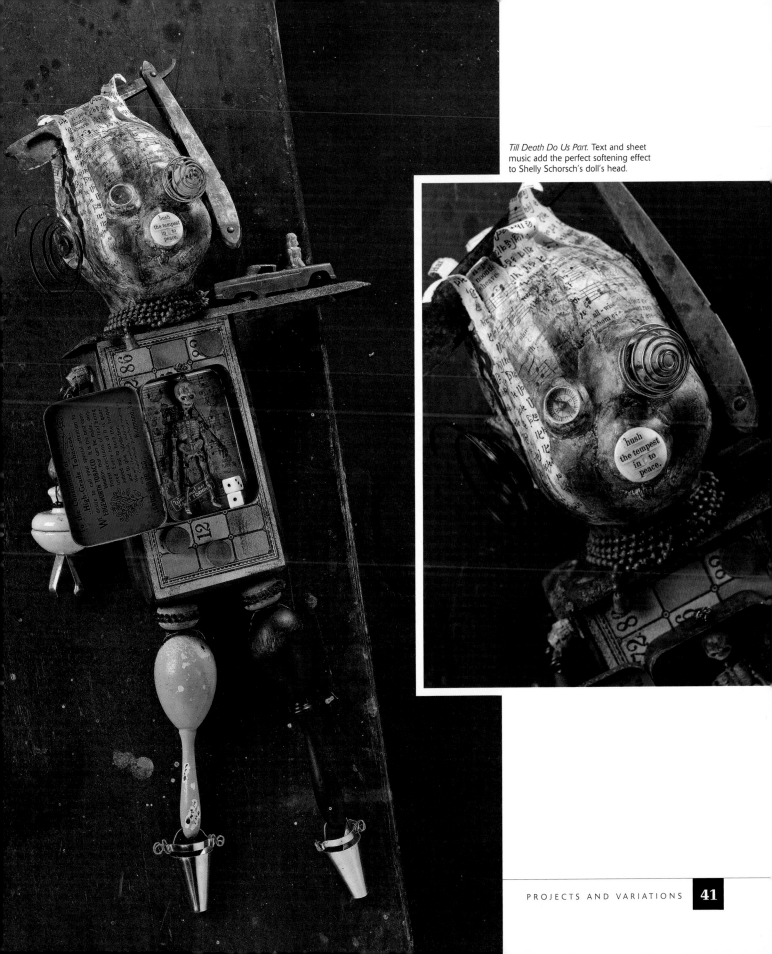

Till Death Do Us Part. Text and sheet music add the perfect softening effect to Shelly Schorsch's doll's head.

michelle allen

About the Artist

Michelle loves the imperfect, slightly eccentric, witty quality of the world around her and hopes that her art never becomes *so* serious as to betray the uniqueness of life that inspires her. Often, if something seems too perfect, she will deliberately skew it toward the unrealistic to capture its whimsical essence.

PROCESS **Baby Bird**

Michelle covered her doll head with collaged pattern tissue. She added a beak, raised the eye sockets and added washers using Apoxie Sculpt. She cut a hole in the head and used an old finial, a soda can top, and an old rubber toy wheel as a headpiece. When the Apoxie Sculpt set, Michelle painted it with a mix of colors that blended with the natural colors of the tissue paper. She used distress inks to color the body. She then collaged Chinese papers and a piece of a Monopoly card to it, and finished the body by nailing antique soda pop caps into it. Michelle's doll's arms are a fishing lure and a piece of aluminum from the lake, which were attached with screw eyes and steel wire.

Baby Bird. Human or bird? Michelle Allen used Apoxie Sculpt to give her doll a beak.

MATERIALS

- basic tool kit (page 13)
- basic project material kit (page 13)
- any size canvas frame, with back opening large enough to house a small assemblage
- gesso (any color)
- medium or white glue
- thin collage papers
- paints, inks, fibers, or specialty paper for additional color/ texture (optional)
- found objects, doodads, doll parts to incorporate into the body and limbs
- found materials to create a double-sided head
- a wood block or piece of wood for the head substrate, cut to size (ours is approx. ¾" × 1½" [1.9 × 3.8 cm]) sanded and colored with paints or inks, or you could use a two-sided clay or Apoxie Sculpt head instead)
- from microfasteners.com: one stainless Pan Head machine screw, item# MSP0216, and one Brass Threaded Insert, item# BT10256 (requires drilling a ⁹⁄₆₄" [3.6 mm] pilot hole)
- 19-gauge dark annealed steel wire, or wire of your choice
- assorted fasteners (we used small screws and washers for the arms and two screw eyes for the legs)
- two pop tops and a small flat bead
- filament to hang your doll (optional)

Dos Dada. A found part from an old Model T Ford gives personality to the face of the authors' Dada.

dos dada

This is a two-sided canvas frame Dada. In addition to Apoxie Sculpt, wire, nails, and screw eyes, this doll features the micro-fastener head attachment.

STEP 1 **Gesso and Collage the Frame**

Gesso both sides of the frame and let it dry. Then collage both sides of the frame with thin collage papers (page 23) and either medium or white glue. We used colorful mulberry papers and, for additional interest, collaged a piece of specialty paper inside the niche and glued fiber to the indent of the frame. You could substitute a thin piece of metal inside the niche as well.

DOS
DADA

TAKE ADVANTAGE
OF THE WOOD
THAT BORDERS
THE FRAME AS
IT OFFERS A LOT
OF STABILITY,
WHICH MEANS
YOU CAN NAIL
INTO IT WITHOUT
DIFFICULTY; JUST
BE MINDFUL
OF THE SIZE OF
YOUR NAILS.

STEP 2 Gather Body Elements

Gather your elements for both sides of the frame and lay out your design. Making the niche assemblage will be the last thing you do, so set those elements aside for now. Attach elements to the flat side of the frame first, using the appropriate fasteners, then turn it over to the niche side and attach everything except the actual niche elements.

STEP 3 Gather Head Elements and Drill the Block

Symmetry plays a major role here, so we selected a proportionately sized vintage wood children's block as the head substrate knowing it would work well on both sides (either clay or Apoxie Sculpt heads are excellent choices as well). If you don't have a suitable block, then cut, sand, and color a wooden piece to fit your frame/body. Drill a ³⁄₁₆" (4.8 mm) hole into the center of the bottom of the block about ½" (1.3 cm) deep.

Audition a variety of items for the face—we chose a metal frame, vintage cabinet photo, mica, and tin can fragments for the niche side and an interesting metal part of a Model T Ford engine and matching tin fragments for the flat side. And we chose a tiny triangular block for the perfect hat. We also gathered assorted fasteners, including small nails, micro-screws, and two pop tops.

STEP 4 The Micro-Fastener Attachment

Drill a hole, ½" (1.3 cm) deep in the middle of the top of the frame with a ⁹⁄₆₄" (3.6 mm) drill bit. Use a flat-head screwdriver to slowly insert the Brass Threaded Insert into the hole. Put a small amount of Apoxie Sculpt into the hole of the wood block and press the Pan Head Machine Screw into it. Turn the block over and press down on it a bit, leaving about ⅝" (1.6 cm) of the screw visible. Pack the hole around the screw with a little more Apoxie Sculpt, being careful not to get *any* into the threads of the screw (a small, thin flat-head screwdriver helps pack). Now one part of the fastener is in the head, the other in the frame.

STEP 5 **Attach Faces**

Look closely at the elements you've chosen for the faces. Select the most appropriate fastener options and attach the faces/elements to both sides of the block. Of course, if your head is made with clay or Apoxie Sculpt, skip this step.

STEP 6 **Attach Limbs**

We selected two miniature bottle openers for the arms and secured them with screws and washers (depending on your limb choices, your attachment methods may vary). The legs are vintage kazoos, embellished with beads and attached with wire to two screw eyes secured to the bottom of the frame. This connection is very similar to the leg attachment in Project 1, except here, the wire goes the other way and the decorative spirals are at the bottom due to the overall nature of the legs.

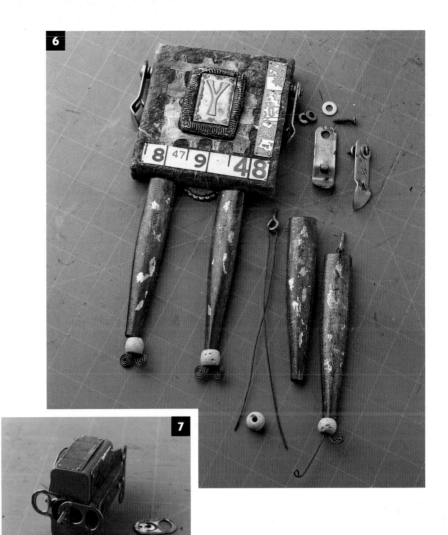

STEP 7 **The Hanger**

When you're ready to join the head and body, choose a thin bead or something similar to cover the screw and simulate a neck. First, however, in order for your doll to be visible from both sides, place one pop top on the head (block) screw. Then place the bead over it and finally the other pop top. If the pop tops need larger holes to clear the screw, use a ⁵⁄₆₄" (2 mm) drill bit to enlarge the holes. Then attach the head by joining the two parts of the micro-fastener attachment.

This unique hanger allows you to swivel the head. You can also suspend the doll, by placing a screw eye into the top of the head or using an existing hole to run filament or fishing line into a hanging loop. An example of this is shown on pages 52–53.

STEP 8 **The Niche**

Once all the Dada elements are attached, the only thing left is the assemblage/niche. Roughen up the surface in the niche, if possible, and apply Apoxie Sculpt. Embed the assemblage elements in the Apoxie Sculpt as desired. Let the assemblage cure undisturbed for several hours.

VARIATIONS

In addition to a couple of our own, the following variations were created by our students during a workshop in Mexico in 2008. We supplied the mulberry and tissue paper, assorted fasteners, and micro-fastener head attachment. Everyone brought their own gessoed frame, specialty papers, beads, and found materials to incorporate. While the basic mulberry papers, which are excellent papers to collage with, are visible, each project is unique to its designer. Everyone received the same instructions as are on pages 44–47 for this project.

Suzanne Sattler

PROCESS **Two-Faced Tess**

Sue painted both sides of her frame with acrylics and then collaged them with pattern tissue and specialty papers in addition to a few interesting figurative images. She added a riveted brass metal panel to the flat side of the frame. Sue made two separate faces from conditioned Super Sculpey and one of the face molds we made during the workshop—she rolled two balls, pressed them into the molds, then joined them together to form a single two-sided face. She put a hole in the base of the Super Sculpey ball and inserted the long threaded screw part of the micro-fastener so it could later attach to the frame. The face was then baked, cooled, and painted . . . each side differently. Sue attached the face to the body so that it could be turned around to face either side at whim. She drilled holes in the sides and bottom of the box for the legs and arms and beaded the arms on wire, attached them to screws, and finished them with acrylic hands. Beading is a consistent theme in Sue's designs. The little wooden legs were attached to screw eyes using glass beads and a wire attachment. Sue then embellished the head with part of a copper mesh scrubby, made a tin can hat, and wrapped a fiber scarf around the neck to hide the screw. The niche was the last thing she did and everything in it was adhered with Apoxie Sculpt.

Two-Faced Tess. Suzanne Sattler's beaded arms make her doll a stunner from either side.

Sue's definition of a doll and artist statement are on page 38.

chelsey kohler

About the Artist

Chelsey was raised on a steady diet of arts and crafts and is lucky enough to be exposed to many creative people whose love of art rubs off on her. No doubt Denise, her mom and close friend, is one of those people with whom she joyfully works and plays. She enjoys many different media and looks forward to a long, exciting life dabbling in art.

> "A doll is any figure that loosely resembles the human form and evokes an emotion in the soul of the viewer."

PROCESS Buzz Off

Chelsey was the youngest person in the workshop and her creative use of materials was very impressive. She made clay faces and feet using the molds, but before she baked them, she inscribed words and premade holes in the head and indents for wire. Once they cooled, she painted them with acrylics and attached the micro-fasteners according to the instructions she was given. She collaged her frame with mulberry papers and used specialty paper inside the niche. Chelsey filled the niche with a watch part and a parasol drink umbrella, from one of our dinners out, which she had cut in half. She then used the other half of the umbrella to collage over a plain wood spool, which she finished with upholstery tacks and a plastic baby, found at one of our favorite bead stores in Puerto Vallarta. Her Dada's arms and legs were constructed from a variety of found materials, embellished with fiber, and attached with screw eyes. She further embellished the legs with fiber. On the other side of the frame, she sewed a key using wire, constructed a "buzz off" bug from resin leaves that she brought with her, and added a heart picture and a bottle cap, which she nailed into the frame. A segment of a wood ruler was secured with additional upholstery tacks.

"ANYONE CAN SLAY A DRAGON, HE TOLD ME, BUT TRY WAKING UP EVERY MORNING AND LOVING THE WORLD ALL OVER AGAIN. THAT'S WHAT TAKES A REAL HERO."

—BRIAN ANDREAS

Buzz Off. Chelsey Kohler used wire to "sew" her key to the frame.

jane leppin

" To me, dolls represent the feelings and issues surrounding both our childhood and our growth into adulthood. They are imbued with all the lessons, fears, and love we experienced as a child, but are also a reflection of the condition of our lives, our health, and our beliefs as we mentally and emotionally work though our continuing relationships. These relationships stay with us into adulthood and even into our old age, where we fondly, or not so fondly, reminisce about the dolls and the unique roles they played in our early lives. In my explorations into the secret lives of dolls, I allow them to express how I saw myself as a child. If I felt loved, then my doll was a beautiful princess. If I felt angry, then my doll was hateful and mean. When I was frightened, my doll became a green-faced monster and so on. And, just as in my childhood, I must play with my materials to reveal the emotions in me that become the subject matter of my dolls. "

About the Artist

Jane says that in a workshop setting, she often looks for opposite ways to create works especially when given the same materials as other participants and strives to make a work requiring its own solutions, knowing she has the safety net of her instructors to guide her.

Born in Vienna, Virginia, a suburb of Washington, D.C., Jane grew up with a creative perspective on life. Living on the wooded family compound known as Wedderburn she has always had an inherent love of nature, music, history, and art. Marrying these interests, Jane enjoys working with pastels, acrylic, watercolor, textile, tools, beads, and recycled materials. The belief that her subject matter needs to be reflected in the medium that best suits her visual expression keeps this artist on the cutting edge of creativity.

PROCESS Celloita: Musica DeVallarta

This doll was born on the streets of Puerto Vallarta as Jane found herself thinking of her daughter Janel, who plays the cello passionately. After one of our scavenger hunts, which Jane says became one of the hallmarks of her workshop experience, she painted her gessoed frame with acrylics and collaged it with specialty papers. As it dried, she molded one face out of Super Sculpey clay and hand built the second face using Apoxie Sculpt. Jane moved on to the first side of the canvas adding images and symbols that she felt would appeal to a musician such as music notes, a butterfly fairy, small bells, and seed beads. The first side went together quite easily compared with the second side, but eventually she began to imagine a young woman sitting on the sidewalk of Vallarta playing the cello. Jane combined that image with her memories of Janel and constructed Celloita's body using handmade paper. For her bow and strings, the artist employed a twig and dried grass found in the courtyard of our Vallarta studio. The arms were created out of old earrings that belonged to Jane's mother, who financed and encouraged her daughters to play instruments. The hands were added later, to fit the composition perfectly. Jane painted and added the legs, which are inverted miniature wooden bowling pins, embellished with wire wraps. The micro-fastener connected the head to the frame, allowing it to swivel, and she used a piece of filament attached to the head, to allow the doll to turn completely so it can be viewed from both sides. Jane feels this doll is as unique a piece of sculpture as her daughter is a musician.

Celloita: Musica DeVallarta. Torn papers create a cello player on Jane Leppin's doll.

"SO, ARTISTS, DRAW DEEPLY FROM THE GOOD NOURISHMENT OF THE EARTH BUT RISE INTO THE GLORY OF THE LIGHT AND AIR AND SUNSHINE. REJOICE IN YOUR OWN SOIL, THE PLACE THAT NURTURED YOU WHEN A HELPLESS SEED."

—EMILY CARR

linda o'brien

PROCESS Nuestra Señora de los Desamparados

The title means "Our Lady of the Abandoned" and this doll features a frame collaged with mulberry papers on the niche side and mulberry paper and cheesecloth on the flat side, then colored with inks. Fragments from a vintage wood ruler, text, and tin were combined with metal and rusted pieces found on the streets of Vallarta and accented with vintage tassels to complete the back. The inside of the niche was covered with Mexican bark paper and features a tiny German nineteenth-century bisque doll that was excavated from the ruins of a bombed-out doll factory in Thuringia, Germany. The crown is made from a washer, a gear, and a very tiny light. Flattened bottle caps, collected on the streets during our dinner excursions, were nailed into the frame and completed this side. The arms are discarded doll parts attached with screws, and the legs are old cornhusking peelers. One side of the head features a polymer clay face using a mold that was made in France and embellished with tissue scraps and acrylic. The other side of the head features an Apoxie Sculpt face. The micro-fastener attachment was used to connect the head to the frame.

Nuestra Señora de los Desamparados. If you look closely, the body of Linda's doll is actually a face.

Linda's definition of a doll and artist statement are on page 151.

MATERIALS

- basic tool kit (page 13)
- basic project material kit (page 13)
- a tin can left intact for the body substrate (the shape and size is your choice)
- a head substrate (we used a rusted can retrieved from the lake)
- found materials for body parts and embellishment
- wire, 19-gauge dark annealed steel or 20-gauge copper
- pop rivets and a pop rivet gun
- detail-cutting tin shears
- a small piece of hanger strap (found in a hardware store and used to support pipe)
- a pop top
- a bottle cap

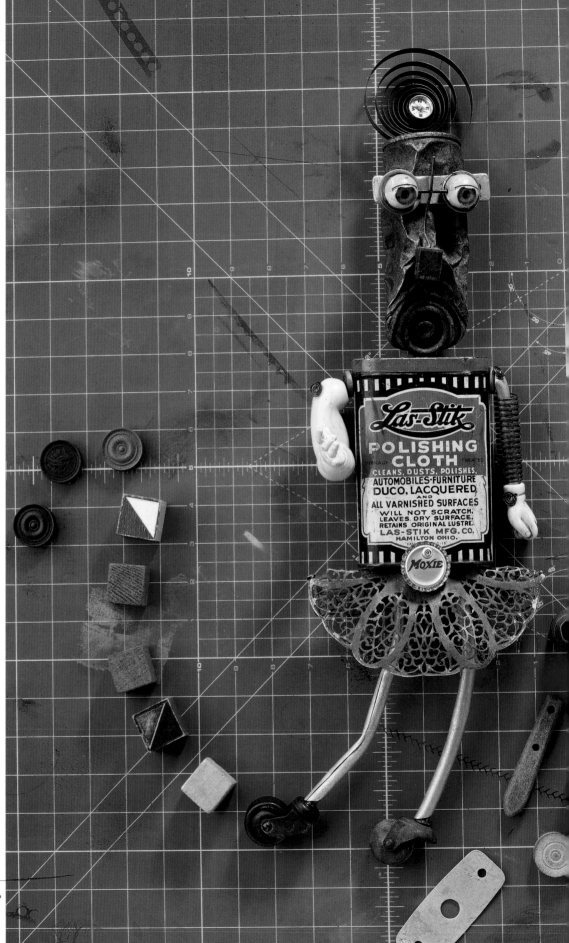

eight, skate, and rotate

Tin dolls were the first dolls we ever made and were the subject of the first doll class we ever taught. We create them using both deconstructed and intact tins and enjoy both styles equally. We discussed deconstructing tin in the technique section, but for this project we leave the tin can intact. In addition to connections and fasteners already covered, this project will include the use of pop rivets.

Eight, Skate, and Rotate. A pair of old rocker eyes give our doll an inquisitive expression.

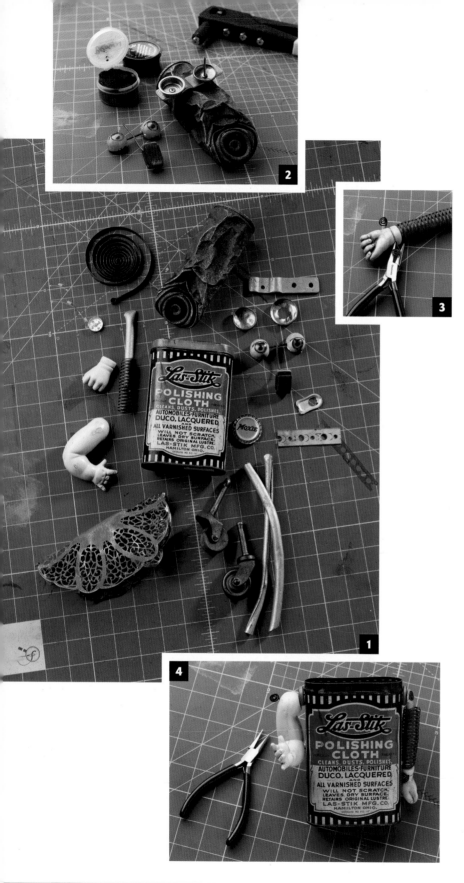

STEP 1 Select a Tin Can and Your Elements

We selected a vintage cleaning tin and a piece of folded metal that resembled a skirt for the body. A rusted, flattened can found on Lake Erie, with additional pieces of metal, became the perfect head. We added a clock part, compass, old pair of doll eyes, a combination of doll parts and found materials for the arms, and finally old metal caster wheels for the legs.

STEP 2 Start with the Eyes

"Start with the eyes" is a favorite line in an Addams Family movie, uttered when Grandmama was serving dinner! Use the pop rivet gun, which has operating instructions on the package, to attach the eyes. Pop-rivet the found metal cup of the left eye to the flat metal piece and the found metal cup of the right eye to both the flat metal piece and the rusted can. Then further adhere the eye assembly to the can with Apoxie Sculpt.

STEP 3 Attach Porcelain Hand and Metal Arm

Our vintage porcelain doll hand required drilling a $\frac{1}{16}$" (1.6 mm) hole in each side of the wrist to accept the wire wrap. Insert the wire through one end of the hand, into and through the metal arm, and then out the other side of the hand. Wrap the ends of the wire in a spiral with the pliers. To form a spiral, make a very small loop at one end of the wire (so the wire looks like the number 9). Hold the loop and tail wire securely in the pliers and with your wrist pointing straight out, make quarter turns to form the spiral.

STEP 4 Attach Arms

Drill $\frac{1}{16}$" (1.6 mm) holes in each side of the body can, near the top. Run a long single piece of wire into one hole, through the can and out the other hole. Secure the arms (one doll arm, one found metal) to the can with the ends of the wire and finish the ends of the wire with a spiral wrap.

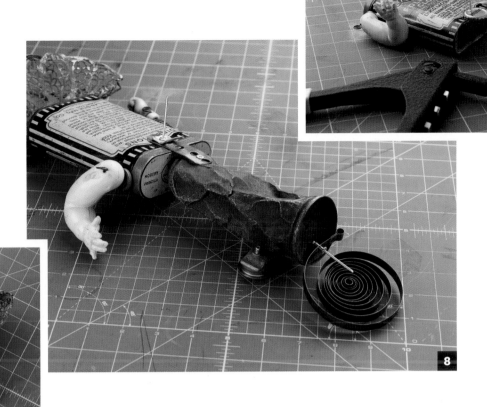

STEP 5 Attach Legs

Drill four small holes in the top of the skirt, leaving a space in the top center so it can eventually be pop-riveted to the can. Drill two small holes in the sides of each of the legs. Run a wire through the legs, bend it, and bring it through the holes in the top of the skirt. Then twist the wire to secure the legs to the skirt. We formed a spiral wrap since it allows the wire to lay flat so it doesn't inhibit the rivet. Attach the caster wheels at the bottom of the legs with Apoxie Sculpt.

STEP 6 Attach Bottle Cap

Drill a ⅛" (3 mm) hole in the flat front of the can and in the Moxie bottle cap. Pop-rivet them together. While pop rivets come in several colors and metals, we used an aluminum rivet since it's the easiest on your hands.

STEP 7 Attach Skirt

Drill a ⅛" (3 mm) hole in the center of the bottom of the can and another one in the center of the top of the skirt and join them with a pop rivet.

STEP 8 Pop-Rivet the Head

Connect the head to the body with the hanger strap. If the strap has holes, perfect; if not, drill ⅛" (3 mm) holes at each end. Pop-rivet one end of the strap to the head and the other end to the body along with a pop top to act as a hanger. Embellish the top of the head with your found objects; we pop-riveted a coiled watch part into the top of the can. A compass, adhered with Apoxie Sculpt, completed the piece.

DOs

A DIAMOND TWIST DRILL BIT, WHICH IS AVAILABLE FROM A JEWELRY SUPPLY STORE, IS BEST WHEN DRILLING PORCELAIN, STONE, AND GLASS. YOU MUST DRILL IN WATER.

The following variations include Dadas that were made from intact tin cans, a deconstructed tin, and a purchased tin nicho. Instructions for deconstructing a tin can are in the technique section (pages 24–25). Three variations are from our students. *Steely the Steelmaster* is a piece created by artist, author, and friend Janette Schuster.

jane leppin

PROCESS Clown

After scribing and cutting the tin support for the head, Jane selected her Dada's face. She wasn't really sure why she chose what she chose, except that it seemed closest to the free floating vision in her mind's eye. She positioned the face with an adhesive sheet and bent the edges of the head around the face to get a more geometric look. The tin/glass box (called a nicho) was purchased and Jane collaged the inside with handmade paper and embellished it with objects that represented her personal interests. The legs and arms were made of coiled copper wire, hands, antique thread spools, and, for decorative purposes, were further embellished with additional copper wire. Jane attached and supported the head using ¹⁄₁₆" (1.6 mm) eyelets in several places. She realized that the doll needed a clear composition line, so she began adding colored brads to the edges of the nicho, creating the feeling that the Dada had come from a carnival. Wanting to further the effect, Jane added brads around the head instead of hair and added small flowers to the hands as well as a key to unlock the artistic secrets hidden within the locked heart inside the nicho. The small silhouette inside the nicho represents Jane's artistic self. In order to soften the effect of the legs in the composition, Jane added strands of torn silk sari. Not only did this add the color that was needed around this area, but it completed the line of composition for which she was searching.

Jane's definition of a doll and artist statement are on page 52.

Clown. Jane Leppin collaged the inside of her tin nicho body with objects that are meaningful to her.

Janette Schuster

"For me, dolls were people-shaped instruments through which my sister and I exercised our vivid imaginations and gave voice to our dreams of adulthood. Through Barbie and Skipper, we tested out possible careers as astronauts, adventurers, and archaeologists. We traveled the world, nursed injured animals, rescued our kidnapped siblings, danced with princes, and occasionally glanced in poor old Ken's direction. You might say our dolls were miniature adult suits we could try on for size. I recently realized that a doll is more than just a child's toy; it can be a medium for creative exploration at any age. I could replace Barbie's plastic body and limbs with a tin can, metal hardware, and found objects. I could cut, drill, saw, alter, and connect these materials to create a kind of metal doll, a robot, that like the dolls of my childhood, is humanlike and through its creation helps me exercise a still vivid imagination."

About the Artist

Janette Schuster is a freelance writer, author, artist, workshop instructor, and incurable treasure hunter. She believes our memories keep the past alive for us. Formally trained as a geologist and archaeologist, she has been digging up artifacts all her life. She now indulges her love of found relics, modern to ancient, by using them in jewelry, collage, assemblage, and mosaics. She lives and creates in rural New Hampshire.

PROCESS Steely the Steelmaster

Steely started life as a well-washed 15 oz vegetable tin with the lid removed, and the open end the bottom of the body. A metal light socket, stripped of the electrical guts and cardboard inserts, became the head. The mouth, nose, and ears were screwed into the socket with tiny machine screws and stove bolts. The eyes are screws, embellished with found electrical parts. A long machine screw inserted from the open bottom and out the top of the socket, housed a combination of washers, nuts, and found objects to make the cap, which Janette temporarily snapped to the socket shell. Janette used a faucet rosette and pipe cover on top of the can to form the neck and punched holes on either side of the rosette rim. She drilled through the punched holes in the rosette into the cover and top of the can, attaching everything with long silver brads. To attach the head, Janette drilled two pairs of $\frac{1}{16}$" (1.6 mm) holes in the top of the can, inside the opening of the faucet rosette neck. She then wrapped two lengths of wire, about 1' (61 cm) each, around each ear, passing the ends through the drilled holes inside the head, and twisted the ends together up near the can top and trimmed the wires with cutters. She then snapped together the socket shell and cap and was ready to make the limbs. The arms are made from two-hole pipe straps screwed into the can with machine screws and hex nuts with attached tiny "key" hands. The legs are 3" (7.6 cm)-long pieces of electrical conduit placed over a wood dowel and secured to the can with matching machine screws and wing nuts. The feet are metal end caps from crescent dinner roll containers attached to the top of a metal storage lid for stability with machine screws and hex nuts. She embellished the lower torso with a hanger strap, pop-riveted directly into it. A metal label, screwed into the upper torso with very tiny machine screws, completed Janette's man of steel.

"TO BE NOBODY BUT YOURSELF—IN A WORLD WHICH IS DOING ITS BEST, NIGHT AND DAY, TO MAKE YOU EVERYBODY ELSE—MEANS TO FIGHT THE HARDEST BATTLE WHICH ANY HUMAN BEING CAN FIGHT, AND NEVER STOP FIGHTING."

—E. E. CUMMINGS

Steely the Steelmaster. A metal light socket becomes the head of Janette Schuster's tin robot.

Suzanne Sattler

PROCESS **Betty**

The doll's body was made from a deconstructed Christmas cookie tin. The face is a fabric transfer that was enhanced with oil crayons and adhered to a piece of tin with medium; the tin was then folded over to frame the face and create the head. The neck and the legs are made from copper hanger strap (used to support pipe) and were attached to the body and head with eyelets. The arms are twisted wire, with tiny silver hand charms attached to it. Sue adorned the head with combinations of wire, beads, and old jewelry parts. The purse, words, belt, and shoes were all cut from various tins and secured to the body with wire. Beads and ornate found metal doodads became the breasts. Some of the tin embellishments were made by carefully cutting pieces of tin so thin that they curled on their own. To do this, take your time and be careful cutting the edges, removing any points or sharp edges.

Betty. Sue Sattler
embellishes her doll to
the nines.

100%
Good

MORE
DOUBLE

Suzanne's definition of a doll and
artist statement are on page 38.

Lynda Crawford-Sheppard

About the Artist

Lynda was deeply involved in musical theater and dance for many years. Life circumstances, family, children, and work prevented her from being engaged in theater. Over the past four years, mixed-media visual art has become a special part of her life and has romanced her artistic center, filling the need for artistic expression that is always there. The act of "creating" brings a real joy and peace into her life and she has a deep yearning to develop a unique and resounding voice in the world of art.

" For me, a doll is a figure that emulates the human body form and elicits comfort. "

PROCESS Doris Bates: Beloved Mother

Lynda used a Price Albert tobacco tin as her body, and began by cutting out photograph faces of her mother at different stages of her life and traced their outline on the tin can backing substrate. She then cut out the tin with tin shears. Using double-sided tape, she secured the faces to the tin with cold laminate. She punched two holes at the top of the heads and placed eyelets in them and attached both heads with a jump ring, so they could flip. She cut patterns for wings from both tin cans and metal mesh and taped them together using double-sided tape. Lynda then punched holes along the edge of the wings and inserted and set eyelets. Lastly, she sewed buttons with waxed linen through the eyelets. The legs are a combination of wire-wrapped crystals with a couple of soldered baubles incorporated into the wrap, which were attached to holes in the bottom of the tin can with additional wire wrapping. The arms were made from sheet metal, cut to size, sanded, rubber-stamped with StazOn ink and etched with etchant. She jointed them with eyelets and attached them to the tin body with waxed linen. As a final touch, a hanger was pop-riveted to the back and a tiny assemblage inside a smaller tin was pop-riveted to the front. When the doll came back to us for photographing, Lynda had added a beautiful soldered skirt using copper tape, 20-gauge wire, and solder. To complete the piece, she applied a piece of copper tape to the circumference of the tin can and soldered the tape. She then soldered the dress to the tin can. Lynda credits Nina Bagley and Stephanie Lee for some of the techniques she learned in their classes, which she used to complete her doll.

"BRINGING THE GIFTS THAT MY ANCESTORS GAVE, I AM THE DREAM AND THE HOPE OF THE SLAVE. I RISE . . . I RISE . . . I RISE."

—MAYA ANGELOU

Doris Bates: Beloved Mother. Lynda Crawford-Sheppard creates a mini-assemblage of her mother as a young girl and attaches it to her doll's body.

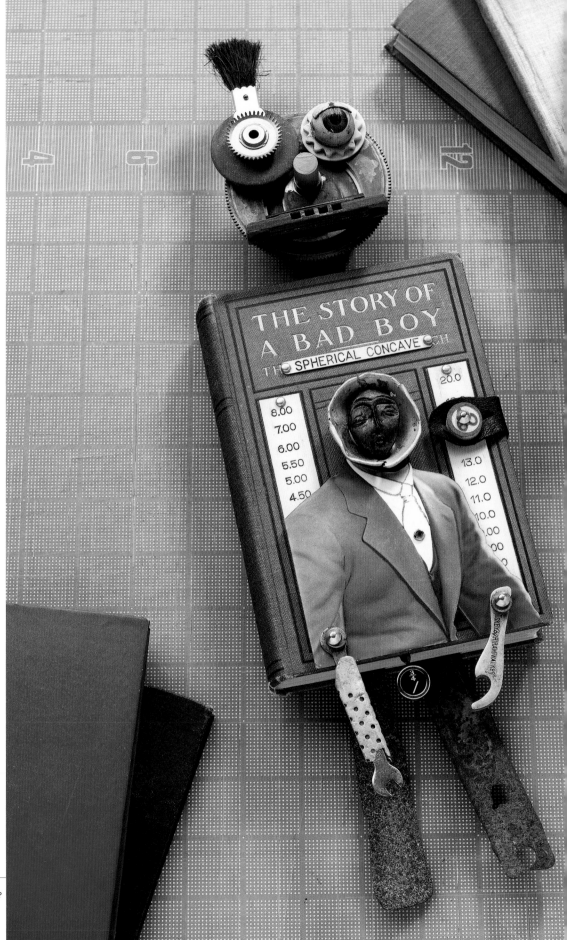

The Story of a Bad Boy. Look at the mini bad boy added to the book cover.

MATERIALS

- ◆ basic tool kit (page 13)
- ◆ basic project material kit (page 13)
- ◆ a hardcover book approximately 5" × 7" × ¾" (12.7 × 17.8 × 1.9 cm)
- ◆ found materials for the head, limbs, and body (yours will differ from ours)
- ◆ embellishments for the body (yours will differ from ours)
- ◆ a photo and a matching substrate to mount it on (thin wood, book board, or foam core)
- ◆ medium or glue
- ◆ wire and assorted fasteners such as small nails, screws, nuts, brads, washers, pop rivets, double-sided tape, and a small dowel piece (your fasteners may vary)
- ◆ wood-cutting saw (optional)
- ◆ a pop rivet gun and ⅛" (3 mm) pop rivet
- ◆ propane torch
- ◆ a piece of leather or metal strapping
- ◆ brads, washers, and a game piece to create a clasp
- ◆ a pop top to make the hanger (optional)

the Story
of a bad boy

We love dolls and we love books and combining them is sheer bliss! We started making book dolls several years ago from rescued hardcover books with catchy titles. We also use the covers of dilapidated children's board books to create layered panel dolls that we pair with themed ephemera. This project features a book we rescued from a flea market. Attachments include pop rivets, micro-screws, nuts, washers, nutdrivers, and brads.

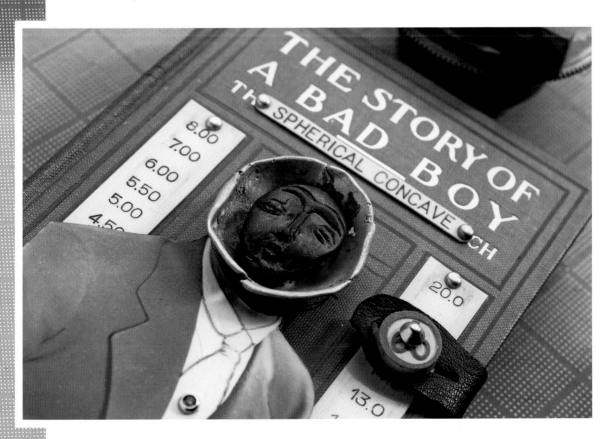

STEP 1 Gather Your Elements

The title of the book dictated the tone of this piece. We selected a variety of found and repurposed materials, including: Tinkertoy parts, an eraser, clock parts, a compass, a toy harmonica, gears for the head, a tiny tool, a bottle opener and scrap metal for the arms and legs, part of a photo of a body, a tiny head that we made, a vintage typewriter key (for his "who-ha"), vintage ivory rulers, a game piece, a scrap of leather, and assorted fasteners. The image does not have to be a paper photo; fabric or imprinted tin would work just as well.

STEP 2 Create the Face

Nail, screw, or pop-rivet one end of the leather or metal strap to the back of the face substrate (the other end will attach to the book later). We used a large Tinkertoy piece as the substrate and attached a large brass piece (possibly a clock part) over it with a small piece of a dowel that fit into corresponding holes in the brass piece and Tinkertoy substrate. We reinforced the dowel join with Apoxie Sculpt. Then we adhered our found elements, such as the eraser, gears, doll eye, small Tinkertoy, and harmonica mouth to the brass piece with Apoxie Sculpt. Your substrate, face parts, fasteners, and other elements will most likely differ from ours.

STEP 3 Add Book Embellishments

We collect vintage optical test lens sets and these ivory measuring devices were in one of the sets. You can use any similar found objects and cut them to size. Position them on the book cover with double-sided tape. Drill ¹⁄₁₆" (1.6 mm) holes into the objects, through the book cover. Attach them with mini-brads and washers.

STEP 4 Attach the "Who-Ha"

To make this Dada anatomically correct, we repurposed a typewriter key. We left some of the "neck" on the key, heated it with a propane torch, and bent it to a 90-degree angle with pliers. While you have the torch fired, flatten the neck so you can attach the key without a distracting bulge . . . enough said! Drill a ¹⁄₁₆" (1.6 mm) hole at the top of the neck and attach the key to the back side of the front cover with a brad.

STEP 5 **Create the Body**

Size the photo and backing substrate so they fit within the edges of the book cover. The backing substrate can be thin wood, book board, thick cardboard, or foam core. You'll need a saw to cut wood, heavy-duty scissors to cut book board or cardboard, and a sharp craft knife to cut foam core. We found a photo to suit our purposes; you can find a photo perfectly sized or resize one. We discarded the original head from the photo and, in its place, pop-riveted a metal disc to the cover and made a small Apoxie Sculpt face to go inside it. Attach your photo to the substrate with medium or glue, then position it on the book cover with double-sided tape. Drill $\frac{1}{16}$" (1.6 mm) holes and attach the photo and substrate to the book with mini brads, tiny nails, micro-screws, or long $\frac{1}{16}$" (1.6 mm) eyelets.

STEP 6 **Attach Arms**

We chose a tiny wrench, a whiskey opener (this is the story of a *bad* boy) and found metal to act as the arms, which we secured with a certain type of brad (called "boobs" from Coffee Break Design) inserted through the tool/opener holes. The piece of perforated found metal was securely curled around the tiny wrench and required no other attachment.

STEP 7 **Attach Legs**

Long rusted pieces of found metal were pop-riveted to the back cover of the book. Brads would have worked equally well.

STEP 8 **Attach Head**

Pop-rivet the free end of the leather or metal strap to the back of the book to attach the head. If you want to hang the piece, a pop top could be added to the strap connecting the body before you pop-rivet it.

STEP 9 **Create a Closure**

Create a closure with a small piece of soft leather. If you're altering or embellishing the inside of the book, do so before creating the closure or it won't fit properly. Make a paper template that extends

from the back to the front cover, shape, and trim it until it is the right length and shape. Use the paper template to cut the leather. Attach one end of the leather to the back of the book; drill holes if necessary. Punch two holes in the opposite end of the leather closure that are spaced about $\frac{1}{4}$" (6 mm) apart horizontally so you can cut a slit between the holes, like a buttonhole, to accommodate the game piece closure. Drill a hole in the center of the game piece and attach it to the front book cover with either a brad or a micro-screw. Slide the leather over the game piece to hold the book closed.

Joyce durand

> "THE CREATION OF SOMETHING NEW IS NOT ACCOMPLISHED BY THE INTELLECT, BUT BY THE PLAY INSTINCT ACTING FROM INNER NECESSITY."
>
> —CARL JUNG

About the Artist

Long before Joyce made dolls, she collected them. From antique stores, yard sales, and junk shops, she took them home, cleaned them up, and gave them the respect they deserved. She believes dolls are a tiny slice of history, a symbol of the place they come from, and the people they represent. Joyce wants her figures to make a statement about their time and place, to "speak" to the people they meet, and to perhaps be discovered by another appreciative collector in the future. Collecting random "stuff" that could become part of a figure is a great joy. Once a figure's personality emerges, Joyce stays true to that vision. She sees new forms and materials all around her and finds using them a most delightful challenge.

> "Humans have always responded to forms resembling or representing their own. Every culture in history has created these likenesses from clay, stone, wood, cloth, and any material available. What we call a 'doll' is a continuation of this tradition, the product of this urge to make something like ourselves."

PROCESS Two Women and a Fool

This book doll is one of the dolls Joyce created during our 2007 weeklong workshop in Puerto Vallarta. Students were asked to bring a small, thin hardcover rescued book with a catchy title. The title of this book and the lead character became the theme. The "fool" in the story was a gentleman from the 1890s. A cookie tin provided an image of such a gentleman, and Joyce attached the image to the front of the book with brads. Arms of sheet foam and precut hands were attached to mimic his posture. Legs made of tongue depressors were painted a formal black and Joyce attached them using larger brads. Coins and beads became feet and were attached with waxed linen. Joyce attached a strip of wood to the back cover to provide support for the porcelain doll's head and a hook for hanging. The head was glued in place on the wood strip, and topped with a found hat, also glued. A sheet foam bow tie and book closure completed the piece.

Two Women and a Fool. A fragment from a tin can becomes the "fool" on the cover of Joyce Durand's book doll.

linda lou horn

PROCESS **Hola: de' Mexico**

This doll was created in our workshop in Puerto Vallarta, Mexico. We supplied a presanded and gessoed figurative board book that had five very sturdy cardboard pages, a variety of imagery, papers, embellishments, acrylic paints, and inks. Linda decided each of the pages would be home to a different doll/personality. She painted, collaged, and sketched an image on each page. For the front cover, she painted and collaged a red dress and background, and cut a red bodice and *Mexico* letters from a soda can and wired and glued them to the book. She sculpted the breasts and face from Paperclay. Linda formed an armature for the hands and arms from wire and used extra-heavy medium to adhere them to the book. For the doll's spiky hair, she cut the bristles off a brush and glued them on the back of her head. The inside cover was collaged with gold foil, with the words *Love* and *Laughter* etched and highlighted with black paint. Pages two and three feature a collaged image of a face with a beaded necklace that was wired in. On page four, Linda's drawn face included raffia hair and on page five, she collaged business cards from our location site, the beautiful Hacienda Mosaico. The image on page six featured a collaged face and painted dress, embellished with waxed linen thread for hair. A collaged head with a soda can for a cap and a sculpted Paperclay arm followed. For the inside back cover, Linda sculpted a flat Paperclay head and added a rusty tin halo, cut from a piece of found tin, which she wired into place. She flattened and painted bottle cap breasts and created a paper and painted dress. Linda then made a wire armature, which she sculpted with Paperclay for the legs and feet. Finally, the back page was paper collaged and painted.

Linda's other doll, *Ms. Lorna Tune*, is on page 124.

Hola: de' Mexico. An open page from Linda Lou Horn's colorful book doll.

Linda's definition of a doll and artist statement is on page 124.

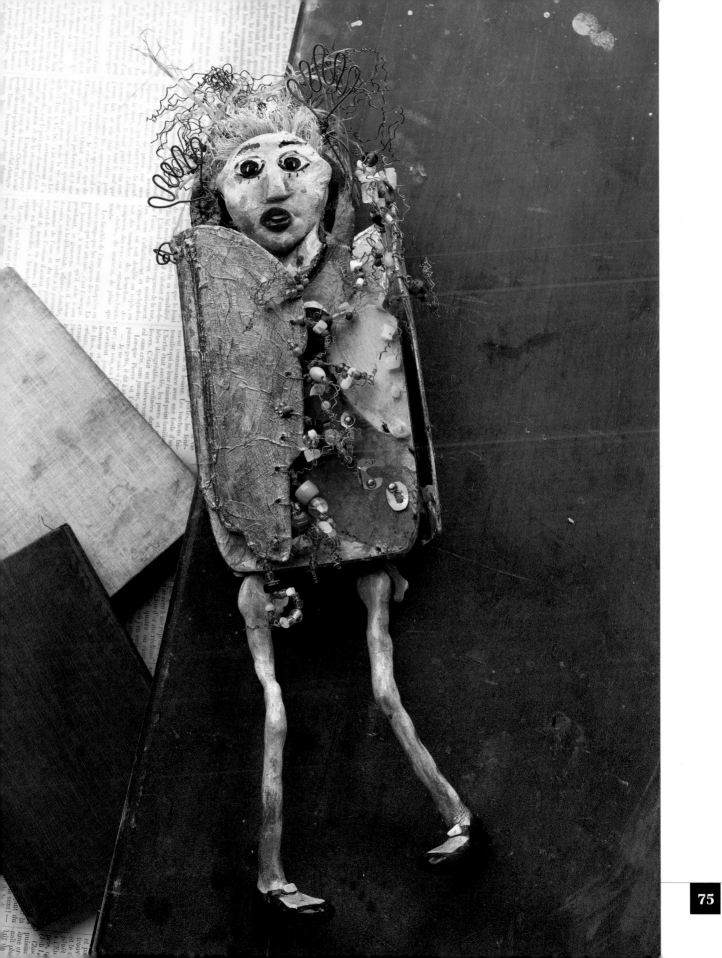

michelle renee bernard

" Doll art—the inevitable result of being a tomboy and not playing with dolls as a child—is the desire to create, manipulate, and otherwise alter small representations of people. "

About the Artist

With a background in graphic design, Michelle spent years "making art" for everyone but herself. When she returned to college to fine-tune her photography skills, she discovered a love of old, worn, and broken-down objects. Michelle eventually moved from behind the camera and embraced antique, found, and everyday objects to create works with visual balance, engaging color, and thoughtful composition. Learning everything she possibly could about all avenues of artistic expression, Michelle found various mediums she enjoyed working with including paper, canvas, fabric, wood, and metal. To satisfy her diverse passions, she often combines them in her mixed-media style art.

PROCESS Angel-Devil

This is another version of the figurative gessoed board book. Michelle thought the girl on her book resembled a wallflower and titled her Dada book, *Loner*. For the first spread she mounted a slide to the girl's head with wire extended into swirly earrings, left the page covered with gesso, stamped random letters in black ink and added embellishments. Michelle was thinking of "Route 66—Go West" for the second spread, so she added elements that would document that journey. The background is a vintage advertisement, with a technique we demonstrated that combines hamster bedding/salt/vinegar for a quick-working patina, which Michelle used on the crown, bezel, and the wings on the Neverland frame at the bottom. The third spread uses an angel image, a fabric transfer, computer text, a question mark, a gemstone at the neckline, and a spade from a playing card as the face, all leaving you with the thought that you never know who you'll come back as; it's just the luck of the draw! She added vintage pattern tissue, a photo of a woman hitchhiker, the rest of the woman's family, aged text, and a compass. The base of the fourth page was stippled with red paint and embellished with a vintage magazine ad with the stamped words *Kitchen Goddess* and *to serve* and a bohemian princess picture on the poker chip, which represented Michelle's kitschy side. The opposite page was inspired by all those "Trucker Rest Stop" places you see when traveling, with a woman, added to the top acting as the book's ambassador and waving a very sultry goodbye. Michelle knew immediately that the devil head was going on the back cover to complete the book. She created the horns from a copy of an old Burma-Shave sign and attached the body and head with Pop It Shapes so they would stand off the page. The arms and legs were attached with brads so they would move. To complete the piece, Michelle stamped *Devil* on one side of the legs, and *Diva* on the other, since she is both!

"NECESSITY . . . IS THE MOTHER OF INVENTION."

—PLATO

Angel-Devil. Michelle Renee Bernard's book doll gets her kicks on Route 66.

gail trunick

PROCESS **She's All He's Got**

This piece is in the authors' collection.

This is a perfect example of a book doll as it showcases the best of both. Inspired by the poem, "He loves her; he loves her not; it doesn't matter; she's all he's got," Gail said the biggest part of making this doll was collecting inspiration in the form of found objects and collage materials. She began with a children's board book that had a drawer in the back. She peeled off the shiny outer page coverings until she was left with thick matte cardboard pages. She collaged over them with worn fabrics, images from old art history books, discarded doll parts, scraps of cloth, buttons, thread, and even snakeskin, creating a book rich in texture and dimension. The figure was deliberately assembled from discarded, mismatched doll parts to convey imperfections and allow Gail to discover who her doll would become. The crude stitching and wrapping of the face and body gives the doll a unique personality, rich in symbolism. The last page with the drawer provided Gail an extra dimension to work with and she approached it as a holder of secrets—a place to hide what is deep within. It houses smaller figures, similar to the doll itself. The meaning and interpretation is left to the imagination of the viewer.

Gail's other doll, *Baby Talk*, is on page 108.

She's All He's Got. Worn fabrics and discarded doll parts bring Gail Trunick's book doll to life.

Gail's definition of a doll and artist statement are on page 108.

The Dada Diaries. Tin left to rust becomes the substrate for the Apoxie Sculpt face on this Dada from Opie and Linda.

MATERIALS
- basic tool kit (page 13)
- basic project material kit (page 13)
- a wood box, about 4½" × 5½" × ¾" (11.4 × 14 × 1.9 cm)
- gesso, paints or inks, and sealer
- thin papers, cheesecloth, medium, and a brush to collage and dry-brush the box
- a piece of rusted metal for the head support
- tin shears
- found objects for embellishment
- doll parts for arms (or make your own)
- instant gratification limbs (we used this technique for the legs)
- a Dada diary (an assemblage can be substituted)

the dada diary

There are so many kinds of box constructions that it was hard to choose one, but this project features several of the covered techniques and also gives you an opportunity to create your own Dada Diary.

STEP 1 **Gesso and Collage Your Box**
Gesso a raw wood box from the craft store and collage it with thin papers and cheesecloth. Dry-brush the box with acrylic paint.

STEP 2 The Rusted Head Substrate

Cut a piece of rusted tin to a desired shape and size for the head substrate. Leave an extra ½" (1.3 cm) at the bottom so it can be folded and later attached to the box/body. Predrill two ⅛" (3 mm) holes into the lower edge of the tin to receive the fasteners.

STEP 3 Mold a Face and Adhere It

Drill a hole in the center of the rusted substrate so you can smush part of the Apoxie Sculpt face through to the other side for a really secure join. Find a face or make one from Apoxie Sculpt and a flexible mold (page 21). Remember to first coat your mold with silicone. Adhere the face to the substrate immediately, while the Apoxie Sculpt is at its stickiest. Let it set a bit before adding definition and carefully embedding objects into it.

STEP 4 Flatten and Design Backside of Face

Paint or rubber-stamp a design on the part of the face that goes through to the back of the rusted substrate for the aesthetics of the piece.

STEP 5 Attach Arms

Drill two ¹⁄₁₆" (1.6 mm) holes in each side of the box as shown. Insert a length of wire from inside the box, out each hole, into the arms. Finish the wires with spiral wraps (page 58) to secure the arms to the box.

STEP 6 Attach Legs

Since the wood is a bit thin, make two lightweight instant gratification legs (pages 22–23). Drill a ¹⁄₁₆" (1.6 mm) hole in each side of the box and insert wire from the top end of the limb through the box and coil it inside.

7

6

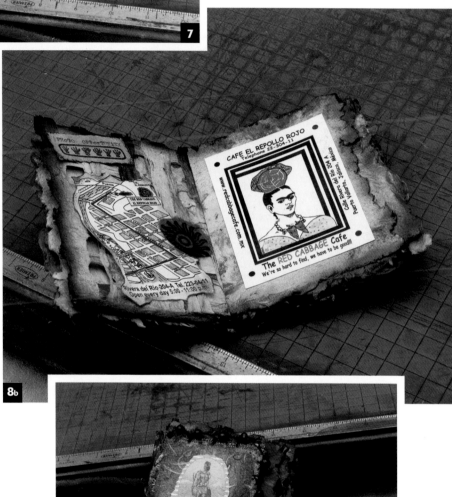

8b

STEP 7 Attach the Head to the Box

Because of the thinness of the substrate, #2 brass paper fasteners and their corresponding washers are perfect for attaching the head to the box. Drill two ⅛" (3 mm) holes in the top of the box to match the two holes in the folded rusted substrate to accept the fasteners. Small machine screws can also be used, as long as the substrate will accept them.

STEP 8 Add a Dada Diary

Refer to the instructions for creating the Dada Diary on pages 26–28. You have many choices for making your diary in regard to cover and page sizes, beading and embellishments, and overall theme. Size the diary so it can sit in the Dada box body. As you can see from the photo, our diary has a Lutradur substrate, a beaded border, and a Mexican theme.

8a

Wendy Casperson

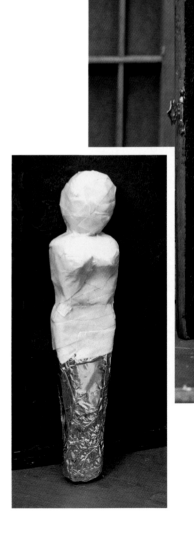

> To me, a doll is any item or assemblage of items that is recognizable as, or conveys the idea of a being, be it human or otherwise.

About the Artist

Wendy has been drawing and crafting since she was a child. Creating was always a huge part of her life. Unfortunately Wendy's muse moved out shortly after the birth of her son Alec, complaining that their studio had been taken over by a crib and diaper pail. Fortunately after a nine-year separation, she decided to come home and is happy to reside in whichever room houses the art supplies. Wendy is a member of the Pittsburgh Book Arts Collective and the Pittsburgh Polymer Clay Guild and works in every media direction possible, taking classes, teaching classes, making art and passing the creative spirit along to Alec, her most cherished creation.

PROCESS Change of Life

The focal point of this piece is a woman's body that Wendy created by compressing and forming aluminum foil and wrapping it with masking tape. She added color by applying Golden fluid acrylics and wiping off the excess with a paper towel. She pounded and distressed the outside of the cigar box with various tools and then stained it using several different colors of Distress Ink pads. Wendy painted the inside of the box with black acrylic and then added pressed and dried red maple leaves from the last fall season inside the box using gel matte medium. She highlighted the outside edges of the leaves with colored pencil. Bones and small pebbles, which she tinted using student-grade acrylics and Golden fluid acrylics, were attached to the box with E6000, along with a found pod, which she rolled in Golden fluid acrylics to highlight the spikes, a branch piece, and a doll form. She painted two small wishbones and glued them over the form. Wendy used a tracing of the form as a template to create a shadow on the inside lid with colored pencil, acrylic paint, and black gesso. She used rubber stamps and the same acrylic paint to add the phrases *Change of Life* and *Life of Change* along the inside edges of the lid, which she then highlighted with colored pencil to complete the piece. Wendy said that the piece holds a great deal of personal expression, through symbolism, in response to this period in her life.

Change of Life. Two small wishbones secure and protect Wendy Casperson's creative handmade doll.

Foil Doll Technique

Wendy was in our Attachment and Devotion workshop at the Society for Contemporary Craft in Pittsburgh. Her young son had been sick so she didn't have time to think about a focal piece for her box construction, and she wasn't even sure if she could attend the workshop. The night before the workshop she made the doll and I asked her if she would share her technique. If you think the instant gratification limb is a great idea, you're going to love this!

This process is very subjective. Wendy created the form with three separate pieces of aluminum foil, the head, upper body, and lower body. For the head she used a square, for the upper body a larger rectangle, and for the lower body, an even larger, longer rectangle of aluminum foil. She started by bunching each piece into the desired shape with her hands. Once she had the general shape, she began to compress and refine it on a hard surface using the back of a spoon. She continued compressing each piece until each was compact and firm; she rounded the edges and pushed in sharp points with a spoon. When she was satisfied with the three units, Wendy lined them up and poked holes, one in the head, two in the upper body, and one in the lower body, using the sharp end of a wooden skewer. She then inserted 1" (2.5 cm)-long pieces of the skewer in the holes, to act as dowels to join the components, with a touch of glue at each connection for stability. Wendy added definition by indenting the lower body with the edge of the spoon or a knitting needle to create the look of legs. She formed small squares into breasts, a semidomed teardrop for a belly and arms, and she added them to the form. Wendy wrapped the form with foil until the joints were covered and the piece looked uniform. She used as much foil as necessary, continually smoothing the surface with her hands and a spoon. When she was happy with the form, she tore irregular shaped pieces of masking or artist's tape and applied them to the foil, smoothing the edges down. She covered the entire form with tape to give it plenty of different angles and then added color.

joyce durand

PROCESS **Kitchen Madonna**

This box construction is a doll Joyce created during our 2007 weeklong workshop in Puerto Vallarta. We provided each student with a wood-based cigar box. An afternoon excursion with her husband to a quaint little nearby town provided the rest. This 1950s icon began as a cigar box covered in pink amate paper. The sweet face and halo were cut from a cookie tin, which Joyce attached to an L-shaped piece of tin with miniature eyelets, screwed to the top of the box. She fitted hollow doll arms with wood dowels and screwed them securely to the back; the screws also supported rings for the hanging wire. Joyce added a plate of tin litho cookies to the open hands and wired a wooden fork and spoon to the bottom of the box for legs. She then painted and fitted the legs with the stylish black pumps that all Kitchen Madonnas wore while baking cookies. Plastic kitchen toys glued to the box completed the image of blissful domesticity.

Kitchen Madonna. Joyce Durand used tin can fragments for the head of her box Dada.

Joyce's definition of a doll and artist statement are on page 72.

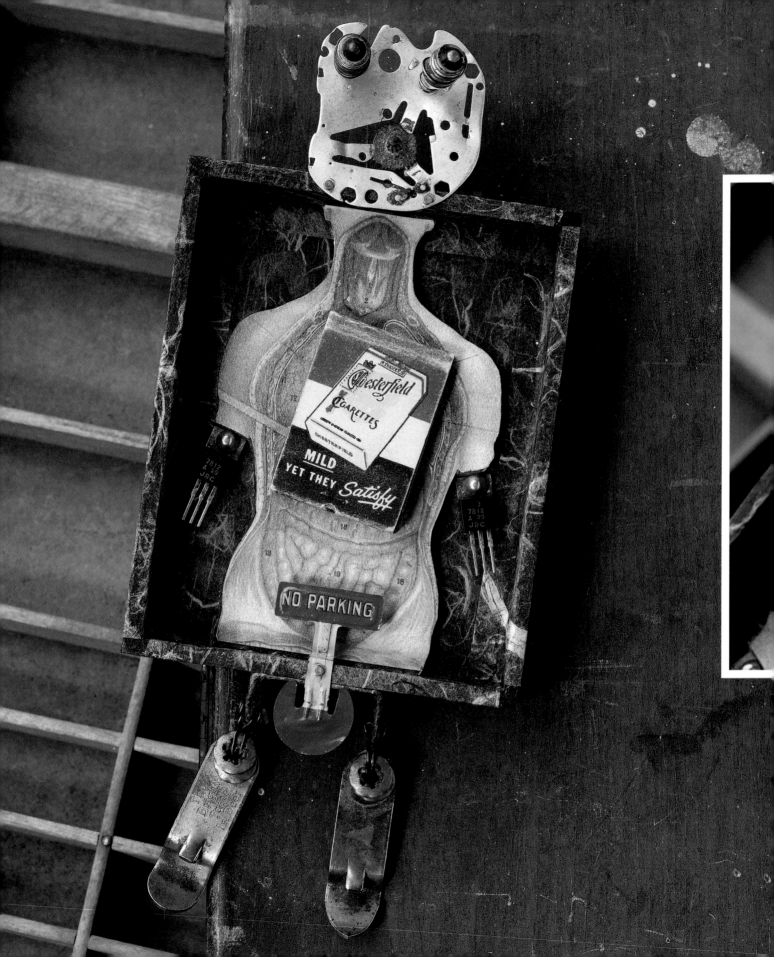

Opie o'brien

Butt-Out. Opie used found objects and the tiniest bulbs ever to create the face for his Dada.

PROCESS **Butt-Out**

Using the same craft box as was used in the box project, Opie gessoed and collaged it. He created a found object head, complete with miniature light bulb eyes that he attached with Apoxie Sculpt. The head, hanger, and "who-ha" (made from a no-parking train part sign) were attached with micro-screws. He chose two miniature bottle openers as legs and wired them to a piece of metal that he cut, folded, drilled, and screwed to the bottom of the box. For the inside of the niche, he colored and sized an anatomy drawing and printed it onto fabric, then he adhered it to a book board and mounted it to the box using PVA. The vintage matchbook was adhered the same way. The hands were parts from a piece of recording equipment, an old 4-track that Opie disassembled after it "gave up the ghost," and he attached them to the box with bauble brads.

Opie's definition of a doll and artist statement are on page 150.

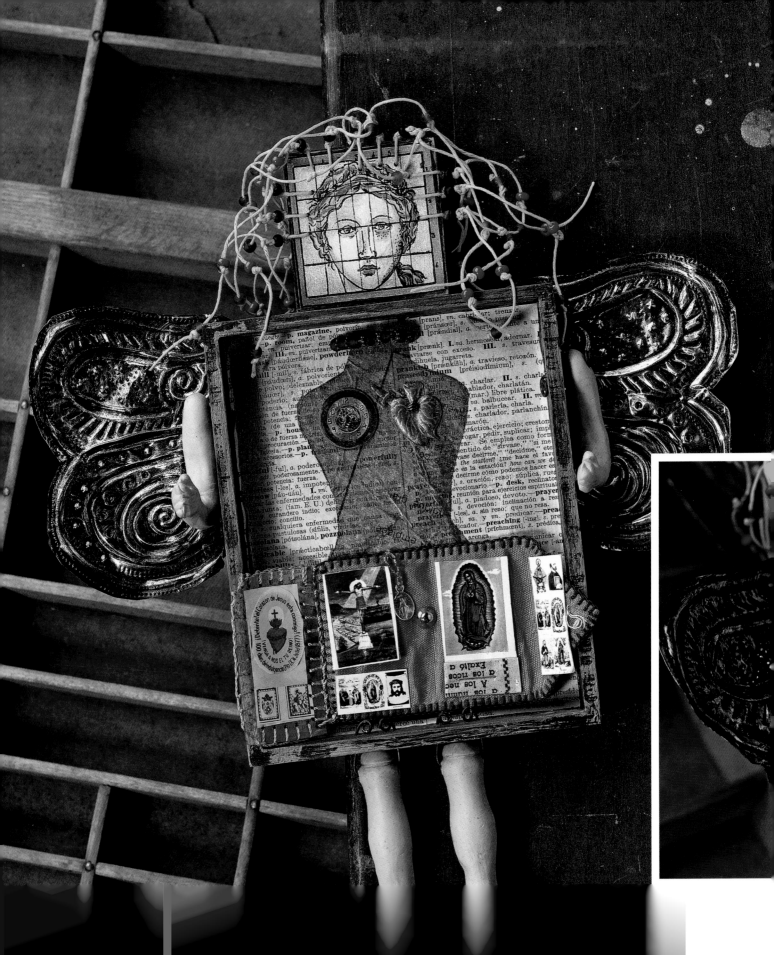

linda o'brien

A Wing and a Prayer. Linda made the arms and legs for this doll from polymer clay, as well as her own molds.

PROCESS **A Wing and a Prayer**

This is another variation of the project box, painted only with acrylics. I rubber-stamped the head using a stamp from our "Doll Parts" rubber stamp sheet, then colored it with pencils, and laser-copied it onto cardstock. I sandwiched the image between cold laminate and mounted it onto a bass wood substrate with double-sided tape. Holes were drilled around the border of the face and the substrate so it could receive waxed linen beaded "hair," which totally secured the face to the substrate. The inside of the box was collaged with text and a torso was made from pattern tissue. I attached the head to the body with wire by drilling two holes in both the box and the head substrate. The wire on the front was beaded to form a necklace and the wire that came out the back was twisted into a spiral to secure it. A hanger was made from a single piece of 10" (25.4 cm) wire, folded in half and looped on the back side, each end brought through the box, through the breasts on the front of the box, and coiled to form "nipples" for a secure attachment. A prayer amulet from a Mexican mercado completed the inside of the box and was secured with a bauble brad. Because I wanted to avoid anything too weight-bearing, I made arms and legs from polymer clay. I made the molds from old doll parts that were perfectly sized for the box; the arms from a polymer clay mold and the legs from a flexible mold-making kit. I drilled a small hole in each side of the box for the arms and two in the bottom of the box for each of the legs and attached them to the box with a simple spiral wire wrap. The wings came last and were made using Pewter tooling foil, found in most craft stores. I drew the design with a stylus and worked from both sides on both a hard linoleum mat and a soft craft foam sheet, to create a raised effect. The wings were attached to the back of the box with double-sided tape and then aged with black acrylic paint.

Linda's definition of a doll and artist statement are on page 151.

Keith lo bue

SPOONFED

MATERIALS: Georgian spoons, Victorian forks, black bean pods, steel wool, doll eyes, steel brads, steel wire, Victorian hairbrush, eucalyptus seed pod, gelatin mold, paper, epoxy resin, soil

STEP 1 After piercing and forming the spoon's bowl, Keith gathered materials that might work as the body (the large pods on upper left and far right didn't make the grade).

STEP 2 An old doll eye mechanism was perfect for the face, so the eye sockets were shaped to fit them snugly.

STEP 3 Annealing, or softening, the Victorian nickel silver forks made them ready for bending into limbs.

STEP 4 Keith dismantled the hairbrush and made brass plates to rivet the fork legs to (the wood was old and thin, and not strong enough on its own).

STEP 5 Australian native black bean seed pods were perfect for batlike ears.

STEP 6 The little man sprouts wire facial hairs and holes for the tacks that fastened the back of the head on (in this case, the rind of a chayote, or choko fruit).

This section concludes with a visual progression of artist Keith Lo Bue's *Odd Doll*. Keith's work with found objects began in October of 1989, and for the past decade he has been teaching others to work with unusual materials in the most creative ways. We have been priviledged to know him since 1998 and admire his work; he is a true original. (For another view see pages 96–97.)

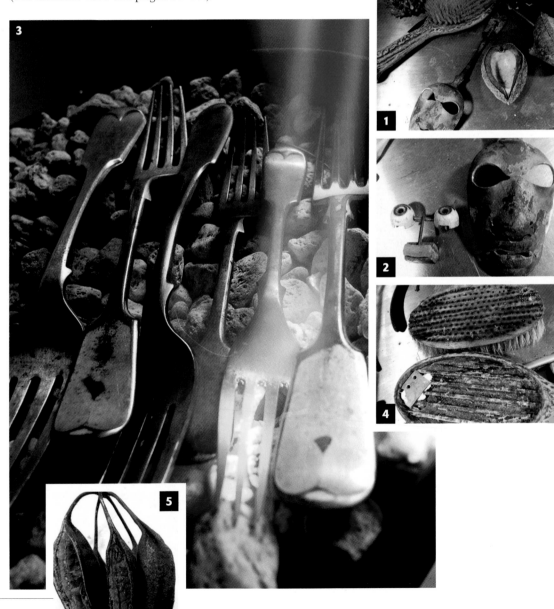

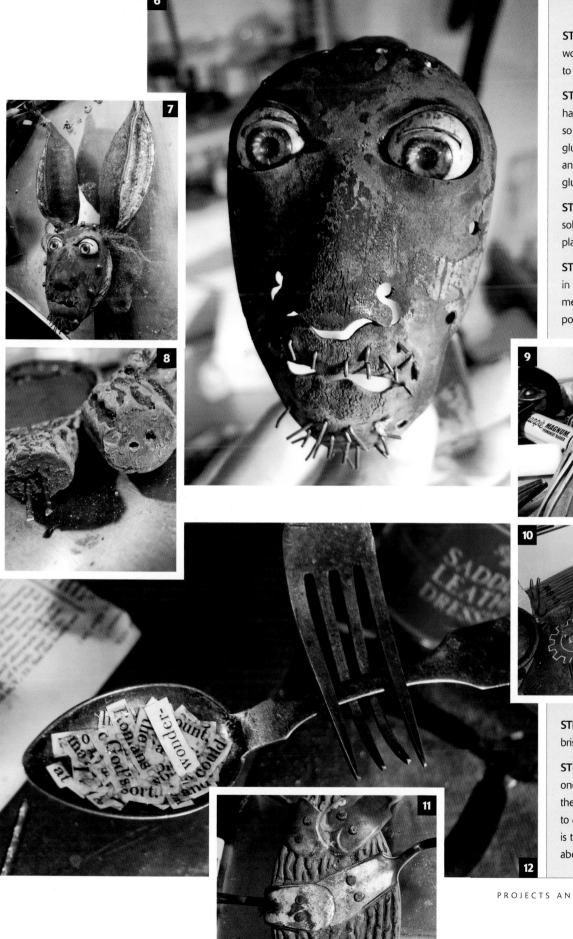

STEP 7 Bean, choko, and steel wool combine with the spoon to finish the head.

STEP 8 Keith cut the brush handle into several segments so it would curl. Steel wire and glue peg the elements together and offer a stronger hold than glue alone.

STEP 9 Fork handles are soldered, bent, and riveted into place under the "body."

STEP 10 Keith put the "tail" in place. The last segment is a medium-sized eucalyptus seed pod, with a spray of steel wool.

STEP 11 The Dada is ready for a bristly back … and some grub.

STEP 12 Keith glued words one by one in the spoon, and then poured epoxy over them to create the "soup." This spoon is the oldest one, dating from about 1790.

gallery of Odd dolls and dadas

CERAMIC PUPPET ARM
C.1350-1500, AZTEC
Found at the Aztec site of Xico
by Dr. Allen Hellin, this deco-
rated art was used on an arti-
culated figure.

Fragment of an
Aztec doll arm

The authors'
collection of
mummy, minkisi,
and fetish dolls

You'll find this section to be much more than a gallery filled with eye candy, although it is definitely that. In addition to an eclectic mix of odd dolls from some of the most well-known and talented artists we know, each of them will give you a peek into their creative process and in their own words, they'll define a doll. What a rare treat! We've come to know many of these artists personally through teaching at creative art venues and feel fortunate to call so many of them friends. The few artists that we haven't had the pleasure or opportunity to meet have been invited because we admire and respect their work tremendously. All are accomplished artists, and many are authors as well, but in lieu of their impressive bios, we opted to include a more personal statement about each of them, and in many cases, a favorite quote. Additional information about them can be found on their websites or blogs, listed at the end of this book. When the Dadas started arriving over a year ago, each day seemed like Christmas and we could hardly contain ourselves having all the dolls together as a group. Each doll is awesome and we are so thankful that these artists believed in the vision we had for this book. Since the project section concluded with Keith Lo Bue's visual progression of his piece, it seemed only fitting to begin this section with him.

keith lo bue

About the Artist

Keith is a master of juxtaposition. His material process is crude and intuitive while he creates objects of careful detail and structure. This dichotomy keeps the creative impulse coursing through him, the thrill of making, married with the spontaneity of instinct.

PROCESS **Spoonfed**

Since so much about the personal meaning of a doll is generated by a sense of character, Keith simply began with a face. Taking a wonderful spoon from the early 1800s and cutting features into its surface, the gruff but inquisitive little *Spoonfed* emerged and demanded the appropriate body (pages 92–93). And some soup.

Spoonfed. A close-up of the expressive face of Keith Lo Bue's piece

Spoonfed. Keith's Dada seems to be asking for some "soup."

"IF PEOPLE
DID NOT
SOMETIMES
DO SILLY
THINGS,
NOTHING
INTELLIGENT
WOULD EVER
GET DONE."
—LUDWIG
WITTGENSTEIN

lynne perrella

About the Artist

Childhood influences and impulses remain a driving factor in Lynne's creativity. She's always considered herself an artist, and an early affinity for making use of "anything in the basement or in Mom's sewing basket" is still her way of working. Simple materials such as paper, glue, string, cardboard, and paint are her favorite materials, and she likes the challenge of using those humble supplies to weave various moods. Lynne's work is about layering and accumulation, and her emphasis is on using lots of materials to create a rich, complex, and integrated surface. Expensive, specific, archival art supplies have little meaning to this artist who prefers to work with "whatever," and finds the possibilities of each material, no matter how whimsical. She challenges herself to keep exploring, letting one idea become the shoulders of the next. She refers to her approach as "call and respond" and tries to work without a specific outcome in mind, always embracing the happy accident.

" *Doll* has always seemed like a shallow and inconsequential word. And yet a better term hasn't really emerged, so I continue to use it. I think *persona* comes closest to how I define the concept of a doll. I work with figures and torsos all the time as a way of constructing identities. Sometimes I like to work very quickly and create something immediate that simply suggests the human body; and sometimes I like doing something quite complex, using many varied materials and adding a lot of research as part of the project. I have been making dolls (mostly of paper) for as long as I can remember, and this activity has always been a great way of executing a fully resolved idea—or providing a very spontaneous lighthearted way of getting started in the studio, as a brain-tickler. Making a doll—I can't think of a better way to begin a day at my drawing board. "

PROCESS Montmartre

Lynne has long been fascinated with the artwork of Henri Toulouse-Lautrec, and did an extensive study of his work in preparation for a workshop she gave in France in 2007. Although most of his paintings, prints, and posters have a natural elegance, his subject matter was the working people of Paris. This inspired Lynne to take a used, common canvas work glove to create the torso for her Dada. She cut the glove apart, turned it inside out, and coated it with gesso. She soaked the glove with acrylic paints and splattered paints on the surface. Lynne stuffed cotton batting inside for dimension, and used gel medium to glue on fabric embellishments. Torn pieces of hand-dyed silk, netting and tulle became the skirts for the figure, and she added a broken fragment of old wire

eyeglasses. Lynne used a photo of Lautrec's eyes to fill the monocle and mounted a color print of a Lautrec painting, *La Goulue Entering The Moulin Rouge* with the figure trimmed out, on cardstock. She tied a narrow piece of black satin ribbon in a bow around the thumb of the glove, to mirror the narrow ribbon worn by the dancer in the painting. Lynne used contact cement to attach the torso/glove to the head and shoulders of the figure. She added more netting and attached wedges of foam core board on the back of the figure to lift it off the background surface. She used a series of paper stencils of vernacular Paris/Montmartre images, including the famous windmill of The Moulin Rouge, plus other typography and lettering from Lautrec posters to cover the background. There is also an image of the artist himself, peeking over the shoulder of La Goulue. Lynne further enriched the surface with deep layers of paint, collage, and monoprinting. Finally she attached the figure/doll to the background.

Montmartre. Notice how Lynne Perrella creatively incorporates the image of the artist himself, peeking over the head of La Goulue.

"WE ARE NOT IMMUNE TO INFLUENCES, BUT ENRICHED AND EMBOLDENED BY THEM."

—LINDA FARGO

deb trotter

"A doll is a soul, in miniature, that honors a life and represents the way its creator sees the world."

About the Artist

A native of the Blue Ridge Mountains of North Carolina, Deb is a mixed-media artist residing in Cody, Wyoming. Using original drawings and vintage photos of cowboys, cowgirls, and Native Americans, Deb's artwork explores the myth and nostalgia of the Old West. Her shrinelet dolls are a mixture of the things she loves—cowgirls, stars, Mexican culture, and handmade paper, all combined with a spunky and sassy attitude. Deb creates, teaches classes, and lives by her favorite cowgirl creed: A cowgirl gets up in the morning, decides what she wants to do, and does it!

PROCESS **Pistols and Petticoats**

This project began with a 5" × 2" × 3" (12.7 × 5.1 × 7.6 cm) cut, cleaned, and sanded wood block, which Deb painted with acrylics. She then cut nine strips of handmade paper to approximately 18" × 1¼" (45.7 × 3.1 cm) and basted the top of each with thread. Deb gathered each strip, and working from the bottom up adhered them to the wood block with hot glue to form ruffles. Once the skirt was complete, a final piece of handmade paper was added to the top of the ruffles for the waistband. Deb purchased a 3" (7.6 cm) tin nicho for the upper torso and computer-generated words to add to the inside. Deb added stars inside the nicho, cleaned the glass, closed the nicho and secured it to the wood block. The 3¼" (8.2 cm) head, an image of a cowgirl, was cut and glued to black cardstock and Deb colored it with chalk using sponge applicators. Then she sprayed it with a fixative, and set it aside to dry. Deb adhered the head to the top of the nicho with pop dots and glued the final embellishments, the gun and holster, to the waist of the skirt.

Pistols and Petticoats. A tin nicho is transformed into a cowgirl shrinelet by Deb Trotter.

judith hoyt

" A doll is a representation of the human figure, a cultural symbol, a prop for a story we want to tell. "

About the Artist

Judith's collages are about old material used to create new work depicted in scraps of paper, fabric, and found metal. She rescues metal from the side of the road, pages from old books, and discarded fabrics from another time. The materials are discolored, corroded, and misshapen by the random process of history—a history that gets passed on to the figures. Each piece evolves through trial and error, the shapes and colors of the materials guiding the development.

PROCESS Shoes with Two Holes (the doll)

Judith's work is powerful in its simplicity. She is a master of her craft. Her doll sculptures are quite large and she starts by arranging found pieces of metal in a pleasing design. She then nails them to ¾" (1.9 cm) plywood and cuts the figure out with a scroll saw and sands the edges of the plywood. She uses oil paint on the edge of the plywood so it looks like the metal on the front. To finish the piece, Judith paints the front surface as necessary.

Shoes with Two Holes. Judith Hoyt is known for powerful, evocative faces made from society's discards.

PROCESS Man with Tie (the necklace)

Judith's necklaces are wonderful. (The featured piece belongs to me.) As with her dolls, she begins by arranging pieces of found metal in a pleasing design. Then she rivets the metal to a copper back and attaches the chain with jump rings.

Man with Tie. A necklace by Judith Hoyt, completely constructed from tin scraps, copper, and rivets.

William Skrips

"Dolls took on a meaning other than girl's playthings after I saw 'The Living Doll' episode on *The Twilight Zone*. The new and very scary dimension that this introduced into my life made me take note of many of the short stories on this theme, as well as the mannequin/ventriloquist's dummy-come-to-life story. When I was young, I really enjoyed reading tales of the supernatural; none of that sci-fi stuff for me, just the *real* scary stuff. The stories I found especially unnerving were the ones where inanimate objects came to life—your basic scare-you-out-of-your-mind, talking, walking doll. I think that this explains why dolls, for me at least, take on a different more sinister aspect the minute you look away. While I don't imagine living characters within the figures I create, nor have I ever (possibly because Rod Serling so scared me with Talky Tina), I do think it's very easy to see the possibility.

To me, the doll is ageless, breakable but repairable, always available, beautiful or ugly, clothed or not, a companion, a role carrier, a trainer for motherhood, gender specific, a toy, symbol, effigy (voodoo, political rallies), and a carrier for miniature fashions and accessories."

About the Artist

For Bill, the use of found objects in combination with carved, painted wood, or welded metal surfaces characterizes his sculptures. He tries to convey an aged, well-worn feeling in his work, underlining the idea that the material used can drive the work. Two forces are apparent. One is the influence of folk or primitive art, with all its rawness and spontaneity. The other is a more formal view, an awareness of modern art and culture, with its accompanying sarcasm and jadedness. The influence of his blue-collar background is never far away, acting as an intermediary between the two. Within the narrative of his work is an attempt to point out the oddities and irregularities of this life, though more in appreciation than in derision or opposition. The result is to pose questions but not necessarily provide answers—much like the paradox of everyday life.

PROCESS Red Shift and Circe: the Digger

While these are two very different pieces, Bill's process is very consistent. His work is about using found materials and pairing them in complementary ways. Often his process is one of trial and error until it comes together for him, however long that may take. In this respect, he must be blessed with the gift of eternal patience. He's a thinker and is always asking himself, "Will this work? Are there insurmountable problems with using this particular object?" Like all of us, he uses the usual attachments: nails, fasteners, wire, screws, epoxies, and even welding, if required. He goes above and beyond doing whatever is needed to get the job done. If an armature is required, he makes one; if a project calls for a carved head, he'll carve one; and if after a week or two, or a month, or even longer, he decides to recut the head for whatever reason and add fabric instead, then he'll do that as well. It's difficult to put his methodology into actual steps since much of his work evolves over long periods of time. But understanding how he "thinks" his creations into being will give you a better glimpse into his very creative style.

Red Shift. This aged rusted metal "skirt" adds depth and texture to Bill Skrips's piece.

"BELIEVE THOSE WHO ARE SEEKING THE TRUTH. DOUBT THOSE WHO FIND IT."

—ANDRÉ GIDE

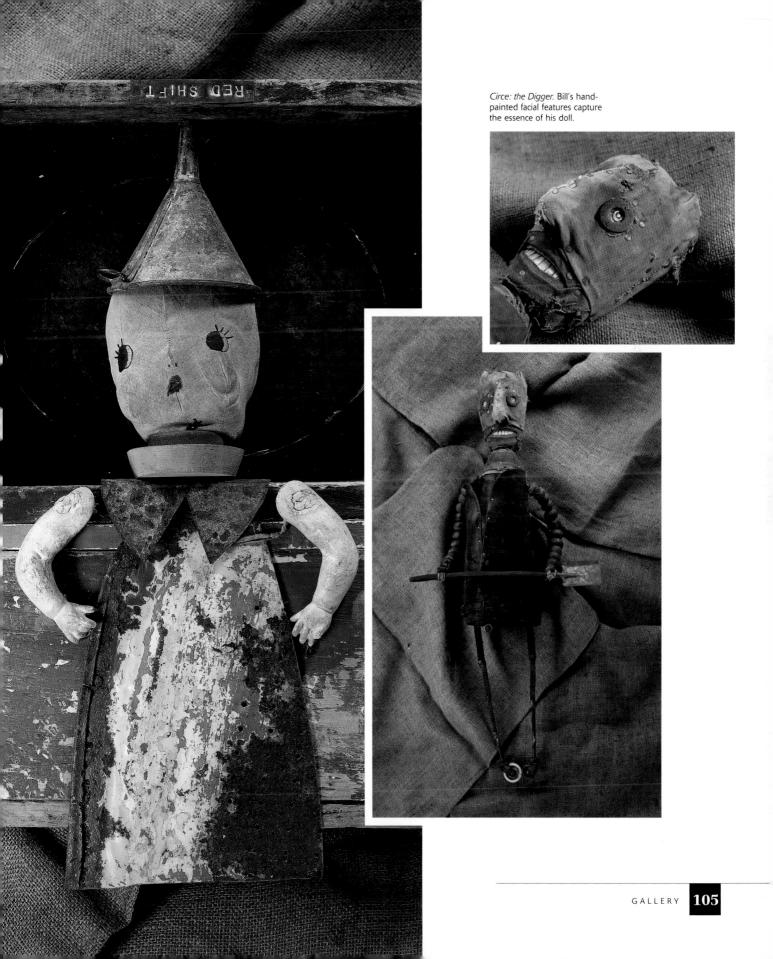

Circe: the Digger. Bill's hand-painted facial features capture the essence of his doll.

Shain Erin

About the Artist

Shain believes artists are explorers who delve into the outer reaches of perception and consciousness, letting their imaginations serve as their compass. Along the way, they collect maps and artifacts, and this is the proof, the puzzle, and the gift they bring back to the familiar world. For his part, Shain ventures into the realms of mythology, moving back and forth through time and space, while standing aside, breathing in the dust of ancient ruins and humming along to post-apocalyptic nursery rhymes. He takes it all in, finding connections in the maps he draws, and collects artifacts that never were. He takes mental snapshots of those he meets along the way and tries to remember every word they say. Piece by piece, Shain is building a secret history of the world, which he expresses through his creations.

PROCESS Mummy Doll (#4 in a series)

This piece is in the authors' collection.

Whenever Shain begins to make a doll, he feels as if countless spirits are jostling for his attention. He tries to get out of their way and let them come through, letting the spirits and materials speak for themselves. The mummy dolls he creates seem so alive. Shain believes mummies are like a book of someone that once lived, filtered through time and weather. He uses Diamond Paperclay for the faces, which is a relatively new medium for him, but one that he has mastered. While it is a bit involved, his unique process results in faces that have the most amazing organic texture. He begins by balling up tin foil over the end of a wooden handle and scrunches it down hard into a small ball with a neck hole. He applies either Grrrip Glue, a craft glue, or he makes his own mixture of GAC200 and acrylic gel medium. While the glue is wet, he applies the clay and begins sculpting the skull-like base form of the face and then lets it dry; he feels this makes working with the Paperclay a lot easier. He works with clay tools and even the ends of paintbrushes to sculpt the details by applying more glue and more clay, using the bone-base structure as his guide. Once the face is dry, he does a light sanding. He then seals the clay with several coats of acrylic gloss spray, which waterproofs the air-dried clay. Only then does he begin to paint the face with acrylics, building up layers until he's happy with the end result. He seals the head with a thin mixture of the GAC200/gel medium, followed with a coat or two of polymer gloss varnish, and finishes with polymer matte varnish.

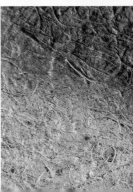

Mummy Doll #4. Shain Erin's use of Diamond Paperclay breathes life into his mummy dolls.

gail trunick

Doll \däl, dól \(noun) 1 : a toy, humanlike in appearance that only a child, or one with the imagination of a child, knows is actually alive.

About the Artist

Gail is committed to going beyond what is in view and toward what she has yet to discover. She considers herself lucky to have grown up in a small town without extra money since this is where she began making things from found materials. The first artwork she remembers making consisted of a collection of differently shaped bottles that she made into differently shaped people who lived in the town. Needless to say, some people were humored, while others were not so happy with the shape of the bottle she chose for them.

PROCESS Baby Talk

The focal piece of this doll is an old metal toy telephone. Gail formed the head, arms, and legs using stoneware clay. After roughly forming the head and extremities, she allowed them to attain leatherlike hardness before carving in the details and expression. She hollowed the head through the base using a melon baller utensil, and cut holes for the eyes using a needle tool. Gail smoothed the clay parts with steel wool after allowing them to air-dry. Once fired, she set commercial doll eyes into the recesses by reaching through the bottom of the head and adhering them with clear epoxy. The head, arms, and legs were attached with an epoxy putty, but Apoxie Sculpt would have worked equally well. Gail roughened her surfaces with sandpaper to ensure a good bond. She achieved the rusted finish using an iron metallic surfacer and rust antiquing solution, available from the craft store.

See Gail's other piece, *She's All He's Got*, on page 78.

"IDEAS ARE LIKE RABBITS.
YOU GET A COUPLE AND
LEARN HOW TO HANDLE
THEM, AND PRETTY SOON
YOU HAVE A DOZEN."
—JOHN STEINBECK

Baby Talk. Notice
how Gail Trunick
seamlessly joins the
doll to the toy phone.

leighanna light

"I avoid using the word *doll* as it conjures up images of pretty, pink, lacy, frilly things and I'm not a pink, frilly kind of woman. My work is about as far away from that as it could possibly be. I see what I make as clay figures, figurative sculptures, art dolls, figurines, icons, statues, spirit dolls, voodoo dolls. Most of the time, I refer to my dolls as peeps or eeps. If I have to explain what I do to someone who has never seen my work, I use the terms *assemblage figures* or *figurative sculptures*. Some have limbs, some don't. Some have faces, but some don't. Most have heads, or something that represents a head, but sometimes not. I see figures in nature, in the bark of a tree, in rocks, in twigs. I am constantly finding 'doll parts' on the ground; twisted pieces of wire are limbs, round rusty things, heads. So I guess my definition of a doll would be an assemblage of objects that resemble or represent a figure or part of a figure."

About the Artist

While Leighanna's background is in fine arts and photography, she considers herself self-taught when it comes to the whimsical assemblage work that she now creates. She loves to create, to hunt for things to create with, and to share her creativity with others, teaching and taking workshops. It's what she lives for … it's her oxygen. She continually looks for unique ways to use and incorporate found materials and is inspired by the beauty of her New Mexico surroundings.

PROCESS Lady Winter

Leighanna likes to keep things simple and divides her process into steps.

1. HUNT: flea markets, thrift stores, estate sales, the ground.

2. GATHER: barbed wire, melted glass, old ugly thin drawer, wooden tissue holder, round-silver-things, fibers, and doodads.

3. PUTZ: sit in your studio for hours rearranging the pieces until they finally make sense, then assemble all objects until a desired outcome is achieved.

4. ALTER: paint the ugly drawer. Apply gesso over a stencil and allow the gesso to dry. Paint several colors of acrylic paint over it and wipe it off gently while it's still wet.

5. ATTACH: drill two holes in a tissue box cover and attach it to the wire. Use the same method to attach round-silver-thingy and melted glass.

6. FACE IT: make a face out of polymer clay and paint it with a black wash to highlight the details. Attach the face and oval shaped glass with E6000. Attach barbed wire under the round-silver-thingy.

7. NAP: take a nap!

Lady Winter. Leighanna Light's polymer clay face gives her piece a soulful persona.

brian andreas

Someone once told Brian that his work is about the edge between being and becoming. There are days when Brian is convinced that our sole purpose for being here is to make up stories to explain what we've already done. Words flow easily throughout much of his work. In StoryPeople, his early and ongoing work with wood and paper, text and image are woven seamlessly together. Each part helps to complete the meaning of the other. Some of his favorite themes are: the mythologies that burn at our core, the fluidity of memory, and the burden of culture unconsidered. But those are just words. You will "see" his work through the lens of your own concerns. So, in the end, perhaps Brian sums it up best when he says he makes art for the same reasons that he does everything else: to be alive and to hold in his hand, if only for a moment, the mysterious heart of the world.

" The first thing Linda and Opie said when they mentioned this book to me was that it was about different ideas of what we call a doll. I've never thought about the sculptures I do as being dolls. If anything, I thought of them as the voices of memory, or stories that speak quietly among themselves, making sense of our lives. When I considered dolls from this point of view, things began to shift. If a doll is a much-loved marker of a phase of life, then this is probably a doll. If a doll is a memory of a quality of life or a moment of time, then yes, this is a doll. If a doll is a confidant and friend, who listens and mirrors back all that you would like yourself to be in your best moments, then this is definitely a doll. So I think of dolls differently nowadays; as placeholders in the world, memory keepers of things we once found important and are unwilling to forget. They are guardians of the promise of our dreams of the future. What better guardian than one who has been with you your whole life? "

PROCESS Almost New Age
This piece is in the authors' collection.

According to Brian, it's all about just messing around! His definition above comes close to describing his particular process. Sometimes he hears a snippet of conversation that starts him on a whole new path. Other times, he'll be drawing on a napkin in a restaurant, or simply watching the patterns of sunlight through the trees in his backyard. He loves brilliant saturated colors (watercolors, acrylics, oils . . . it really doesn't matter) and the way piles of random scraps in the wood shop can become a body, or an arm, or a leg with the addition of paint or wire. And words. Words of all types, but especially simple words that everyone knows. He loves the way that simple words, arranged in a new way, can unlock the cage of your own mind, so that you can begin to trust your heart. Of course, there's the technical stuff, like practice, materials, production, and endless repetition—all crucial to his process. Brian uses wood from century-old homesteads in northeast Iowa, tin from the roofs of dilapidated barns, rusted wire from construction sites—stuff with history; stuff that had its own life in the world before he found it. Brian's stories are originals, taken from his experiences and those of his family and friends. You'll notice that his stories are quite short. He's heard them called Western haiku. There's actually a simple technical reason for this: they're hand-stamped, one letter at a time, which Brian says is a marvelous incentive for keeping them brief. They are hand-stamped because the wood he uses is old and weathered and requires constantly adapting the surface in order to get a legible letter. In the end, it's all a dance and it's the thing that keeps him interested and coming back for more.

Is willing to accept that she creates her own reality except for some of the parts where she can't help but wonder what the hell she was thinking.

Almost New Age. Brian Andreas hand-stamped this doll's story, one letter at a time.

linda drake

" First of all, it's very liberating to toss out all of your preconceived notions of commercial dolls. Taking unrelated objects and creating an art doll brings out huge sacred energy. Taking a commercial doll and removing all of its surface decoration including the hair, allows you to go beneath the surface and bring out the real soul of the doll. It's like removing your makeup and clothes and standing naked in front of a mirror! I think creating art dolls brings out the true intent of what dolls were originally meant to be—representations of our spirits that speak to all of us. "

About the Artist

Linda, a full-time artist, works mainly in mixed media. She loves creating assemblage, shrines, and dolls. Lately she's been working with canvas, using lots of paint, fabric, old papers, books, and dictionary pages. She enjoys recycling, repurposing, and incorporating found materials. Being self-taught, she lets her art evolve on its own, leading her down paths of discovery and enlightenment. Her art is always upbeat and happy, mirroring her general mood. Linda believes that seeing someone connect with your art is the ultimate gift of creating.

PROCESS Road to Love

Linda's doll could have comfortably fit into the book or canvas category. She began by covering four 4" × 4" (10.2 × 10.2 cm) frames with pages from an old romance book, using gel medium. When dry, she brayered on white acrylic paint and Golden's mustard yellow glaze and then randomly applied pattern tissue to the surface. Using staples, she joined the frames into a one-piece "U" shape and moved on to create the doll. Linda took a ½" (1.3 cm)-thick section from the same book and first cut the torso top and then the skirt. Punching holes in the mid-section of both pieces, she bound them together with elastic cording. She cut the arms and legs from ¼" (6 mm)-thick pages and bound them together with white button thread. She lifted the skirt and screwed the lower skirt body to the frame and cut the remaining skirt in layers for a more dimensional look. To solidify the torso and skirt, Linda used beeswax. Small jewelry tags with positive affirmation words were added to the skirt. She cut the head and wings from an old rusted tin, and joined the head, arms, and legs with pop rivets. Then, she made a hanger from an old metal wire shaped into a zigzag to arch over the top, which she attached to the sides of the frame with upholstery tacks. A bottle cap filled with paper and bits of fabric strips completed the hanger. To finish the piece, Linda took the words *The Road to Love* from the back of the spine and collaged them to the piece.

> "IT'S NOT HARD WORK THAT WEARS YOU OUT BUT THE REPRESSION OF OUR TRUE PERSONALITY."
> —UNKNOWN

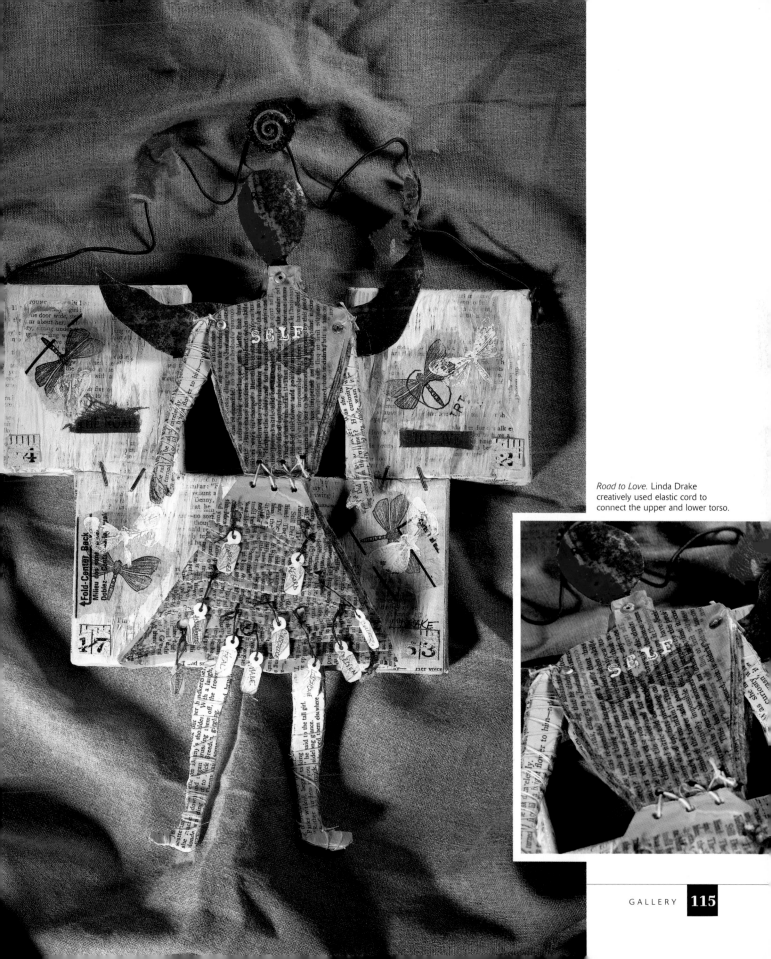

Road to Love. Linda Drake creatively used elastic cord to connect the upper and lower torso.

terry taylor

" Boys aren't supposed to like dolls, nor are we encouraged to play with them. I wasn't like other boys. I eagerly anticipated visiting my girl cousins, who would invite me to play with them *and* their dolls. Dressing dolls, make-believe play, sewing clothes: what's not to like? And, truth be told, I did have a baby doll named Ruthie (still do) and a fashion doll that my mother made a trunkful of clothes for one Christmas. Also, I was lucky to be introduced to doll forms that didn't fit the usual mold. When I lived overseas as a child, I was given a pair of Japanese *kokeshi* dolls. Their simple form—a round head and cylindrical torso—was unlike anything I had seen before, but I understood innately that these dolls were sufficient when paired with my imagination. I was also entranced by the sacred figures tinged with gold that were stored in a cabinet in our military church building. They were mysterious and forbidden: what were they for, who were they, and why couldn't we have them in our services? I don't often use the doll form, but elements of the human form are ever present in my work. "

About the Artist

Terry creates all sorts of work in many different mediums. He is a senior editor for Lark Books and has authored books on a wide variety of subjects. He lives with a lot of art and many, many things in boxes, binders, and stacks. All of his things inspire him in different ways. When asked how he works, he says, "I compose, juxtapose, take things out of context, or give things new contexts. I'm not a prolific or especially fast worker, though I do have blissful bouts when something I'm working on comes together quickly. More often than not, pieces and parts sit unfinished or unassembled for a long while, until a little voice tells me what to do. I'm patient and a firm believer in letting the unconscious sort everything out. I like things. I like to make things. Sometimes I think I've made art. Sometimes I've just made that thing."

PROCESS Untitled

Terry rarely has a finished object in mind when he begins a piece, he prefers to work slowly by accretion and happenstance. He used to troll flea markets for materials, but now he goes online searching for inspirational objects. He searched for porcelain doll heads and went on a judicious bidding spree. Male heads were few and far between. Alas, his favorite head met an untimely demise (I wonder how . . .) but fortunately he had a couple of others to choose from. The idea of painting one of the heads with china paint was considered and quickly abandoned. Terry decided to create a steel wire framework to mimic old *Santos* (a New Mexican genre of religious sculpture), especially the ones with framework torsos that were dressed in hand-sewn robes. He created a stand with a stash of odd wooden blocks with painted markings that were perfect to support the wire form. He decided to attach the head and other items with a combination of simple loops and wire wraps, which really complemented the piece. A doll arm search produced a mother lode of relatively inexpensive vintage porcelain arms. He then drilled holes in a pair of porcelain hands with a diamond-coated drill bit and enlarged the holes in the upper porcelain arms. The iconic image in the tart form came from a vintage exercise book. Terry gave the image a coat of beeswax, added a string of vintage seed beads and heated the beeswax to hold the beads and the diabolical mask. The little plastic head and red beads worked well together. He added *milagros*, machine-flattened pennies with praying hands motifs, and biblical text left over from a previous project. A hand-cut steel Masonic emblem completed the back of the figure and contrasted with the arms in an angelic sort of winglike way. The rest, he said, would be left to the imagination of the viewer.

Untitled. A vintage waxed drawing complete with devil's head resides in a tiny tart tin within Terry Taylor's *Santos.*

clarissa callesen

" I see dolls as inanimate creations that symbolize our human existence. Often small and overlooked in the fine art world, they are powerful talismans and reflections of our dreams, our pain, our helplessness, and our joy. "

About the Artist

Clarissa Callesen is a former rodeo princess who left behind her bleached blond hair and big earrings (at least most of the time) for the wild ride of life as an artist. She started her artistic career as a tattoo artist, creating unique personal statements on people's skin. Over the years she has worn several hats and eventually the cool quiet of clay replaced the buzz of the tattoo gun. Tattoo imagery, religious icons, and an out-of-control junk collection took her headlong into the exciting world of mixed-media assemblage. Today she has found a happy marriage combining assemblage with her love of ceramic sculpture.

PROCESS Frida's Lost Doll

This piece is in the authors' collection.

When I first saw this doll I was drawn to it and purchased it for my collection of special artist dolls that adorn the walls of my studio. Needless to say, my studio is filled with a wonderful energy, very conducive to creativity.

Many of Clarissa's pieces start with a random collection of favorite things that more often than not reveal their intent through the process of creation. This piece grew out of an old ceramic electrical insulator, a piece of old wood, and some scraps of ceramic clay that reminded Clarissa of wings. She collaged the base, a broken piece of wood, with a fragment of aged paper that added both a subtle layer of texture and addressed the broken rough edge of the wood. Clarissa constructed the main doll body on the bottom of an Altoids gum tin that had been rusted and turned upside down. She attached the ceramic insulator with Liquid Nails and adhered a small ceramic face to the nail that ran through the insulator to create the doll's head. The skirt came next. The top layer is a paper drink parasol cut in half and stained with walnut ink and the main layer is a torn piece of stained fabric. To add more movement and texture, Clarissa added irregular pieces of string between the skirt layers. She attached ceramic scrap wings and rusty nails to suggest arms. Interesting electrical capacitors gave the head a sort of aura. She glued a piece of scrap wood into the void of the upside-down tin to create a larger surface for connection, and then glued the entire doll, on the tin, to the wood substrate. Clarissa's finishing touches included pieces of plumber's tape cut into shapes to frame the top and bottom of the doll, a small wooden animal, a metal flower, and buttons. Finally, she added thin layers of acrylic paint mixed with matte gel medium to unify the piece with a semitranslucent finish and dark brown paint, blended with the Liquid Nails, to camouflage the connections.

> "NORMAL IS NOT SOMETHING TO ASPIRE TO; IT'S SOMETHING TO GET AWAY FROM."
> —JODIE FOSTER

Frida's Lost Doll. The body of Clarissa Callesen's doll began life as an old ceramic electrical insulator.

diane kurzyna
a.k.a. ruby re-usable

"A doll is a window into another world. Much more than a plaything, it embodies the passing down of cultural traditions, mirroring the society that created it and representing the values of the giver."

About the Artist

As a child, Diane loved her dolls and made clothes and environments for them out of fabric scraps, rubber bands, shoe boxes, tape, and other odds and ends. Today she collects dolls that intrigue her, mostly by rescuing them from Goodwill and giving them a good home. She loves dolls made from unusual materials or from exotic locales and feels dolls embody our sense of community, connecting us to other times, other places, and other people. Creating dolls out of recycled materials is a craft that celebrates human ingenuity, while calling attention to human excess. Our foremothers used cornhusks, rags, or whatever was available to craft dolls and it is in that same spirit that Diane creates hers. Her intent is to transform human-generated waste into something interesting, revealing value in what society has deemed worthless, and beauty where it is least expected.

PROCESS Sweetheart Baby

This piece is in the authors' collection.

This doll is one of the signature Plastic Bag Babies that Diane is so well known for. It's made from repurposed plastic bread bags, stuffed with used bubble wrap, and held together with clear tape. While no babies were harmed during the creative process, the manufacturing of plastic is a harmful process that is unhealthy to all living things and another reason why we should all recycle. Diane uses a baby doll from Goodwill as a mold and says the best doll to use has a plastic head, arms and legs, and a cloth body. Once she selects her plastic bag, she cuts it open to lie flat. Depending on the graphics you want to be visible, and the size of your doll, you may need more than one bag. Cut a rectangular strip from the bag so it will completely cover one of the arms, then repeat for the other arm. With thin strips of clear tape, wrap the plastic strip around the arm and hold it in place with tape, being careful not to put tape on the doll, just the plastic, and repeat for the other arm. Do the same for both of the legs. Next, cut a rectangular strip to cover the head and body, front and back. You can cut several pieces of plastic, holding them together with tape. The piece should be wide enough to cover the sides as well as the front of the doll, but if it isn't, you can cover the sides separately. Smooth the plastic bag around the front and back of the head and tape it tightly at the neck, then tape the arms and legs to the body piece. Then, wrap wide tape around the waist, under the neck, around the belly to between the legs and up the back, ending underneath the head. Cover the entire doll with tape using thick and thin strips (whatever works) until every surface is covered. Two layers of tape are plenty. Lastly, remove the doll from the plastic bag by cutting one vertical cut/line down the back, from the head to the tush, with scissors and carefully pulling the mold out. Stuff the form with small pieces of bubble wrap, starting with the extremities, then the head, and finally the body. When the doll is well stuffed, tape it back up again.

Sweetheart Baby. A plastic bag from a loaf of sweetheart bread is transformed in Diane Kurzyna's hands.

eric allen montgomery

" I know that historically dolls have been made from just about everything: bone, antler, twigs, cornhusks, clothes pegs, you name it, and that many museum samples (and several contemporary examples) bear little resemblance to the human form. Yet in my mind, a doll must at least have *some* anthropomorphic qualities. I think of dolls as something, or some*one*, to play with, to talk to, to interact and communicate with in some way, unlike a figurative sculpture. Therefore, in my definition, and in the various dolls I have created and continue to create, there must be a face to connect with, however removed from actual 'human' representation that may be. It could be a clock face or a gear or gauge, or simply something that only vaguely suggests a face—but something to *connect* with visually and mentally, to focus my interaction upon. "

About the Artist

Eric Allen Montgomery is a mixed-media sculptor and glass artist who recently moved to Guelph, Ontario, from the West Coast of British Columbia, Canada. He plays with vintage toys and tools, old photos and fragments, and rusty bits to create his unique award-winning, mixed-media memory boxes, available primarily by commission or through select galleries. He utilizes a wide variety of found, altered, and created objects and materials to celebrate events, interpret themes, or simply to tell stories, both real or imagined. Eric's diverse technical background and inherent eye for color, texture, and balance are well used in this marriage of materials. Form and function combine with reality and myth, linking the technical expertise of a craftsperson, the aesthetic and philosophical explorations of an artist, and the wit and whimsy of a storyteller.

PROCESS Mad Saint Louis

Most of *Mad Saint Louis* is composed of "as is" found objects. His head is a rusty cage for protecting a work light, that is stamped "St. Louis." His face is the broken remains of a china doll. The eyes had been held in place with plaster, and popped out whole, so you can see them . . . just as they see you. His body is a rescued drawer from an old hardware store where Eric's dad purchased a large collection of drawers filled with vintage MG car parts, and after removing the parts, planned to take the drawers to the dump, when Eric rescued them. Eric painted the interior of the drawer with acrylics and top-coated it with a spackling compound that gives the impression of plaster skin; otherwise, the drawer is "as it was found" including labels and scribbled penciled notes from its hardware days. The Dada's "wings" are antique brackets for hanging plants or oil lamps, his "lungs" a found bottle with a leaf skeleton already inside; alarm clock ticker, various gauges, tubes, and Christmas lights complete the body. His arms are vintage fishing weights, a paintbrush and fork, along with a copper prayer token. Eric used a vintage folding ruler for the legs. Eric only had one wooden shoe for a foot, when somehow the concept of a "club foot" popped into his head—he used a nine of clubs playing card. Eric's means of delivering the *Spark of Life* is courtesy of NGK (the manufacturer) and is very creative. With the exception of the box interior, the Dada came together with screws, glues, and a few drilled holes. Eric prefers to use what he calls "The Patina of Life," the natural surfaces of old objects created by time and wear, rather than any faux finishing techniques.

> "PEOPLE DON'T KNOW WHAT THEY WANT, NOT BEFORE THEY SEE IT. EVERY OBJECT OF DESIRE IS A FOUND OBJECT. TRADITIONALLY, ANYWAY."
>
> —WILLIAM GIBSON

Mad Saint Louis. A broken china doll head and eyes encased in plaster invite you to delve deeper into Eric Allen Montgomery's Dada sculpture.

linda lou horn

"A doll is a three-dimensional figurative sculpture, human, animal, ethereal, or any combination thereof, which evokes memory, emotion, dialog, and relationship."

About the Artist

Linda's intent is to be open to discovery and surprise herself by making something she's never seen before. She is excited by non-art materials, old objects, and found materials that have had a previous life and are not intended for the purpose she gives them. The human condition, memories, emotions, relationships, pain and laughter, and spirited aliveness, inspire her. She is a daughter of a rubbish hauler; she loved riding in the truck with her dad and going to the city dump, finding richness in trash as raw materials for making something new with worth, value, and meaning. Her forty-plus years as a nurse and psychotherapist have helped her see the possibilities and the best in all that has been broken, lost, or abandoned and hopes her art reflects this.

PROCESS Ms Lorna Tune

This piece began with a white 1960s Fisher Price toy xylophone. Linda discarded the plastic wheels, removed the metal notes, then distressed, primed, and painted it in yellows and reds. When everything was dry she replaced the metal notes. She then cut four vintage chair legs, drilled a hole in the bottom of each and glued in four vintage caster wheels. Each leg was screwed into the bottom of the xylophone with wood screws. For the tail, Linda cut the handle off a stiff, used paintbrush, repainted it, drilled a hole in both the body of the xylophone and the brush and joined them with wire and glue. She painted and glued together two round wooden discs and balls and screwed and glued them onto the front of the toy. She made a mallet from a dowel and a round ball and painted it, then attached tacks to the side of the toy, to slide/hold the mallet in place. An old broom with a wooden handle formed the armature for the head and neck and Linda proceeded to create the head with Original Paperclay. See the sidebar for details.

She added curly doll hair around the straw hair baseline and a pair of vintage musical instrument earrings. Linda used a length of a broom handle to attach the head/neck to the body, fitting it to a soup bone at the base of the neck, and adhering it with epoxy. Lastly, she drilled a hole through the first metal plate/note on the xylophone and then through the soup bone and used a 2 ½" (6.4 cm) screw to position the head.

Linda's other piece, *Hola De Mexico*, is on page 74.

Ms Lorna Tune. Original Paperclay and an old broom form the head of Linda Horn's very funky xylophone doll.

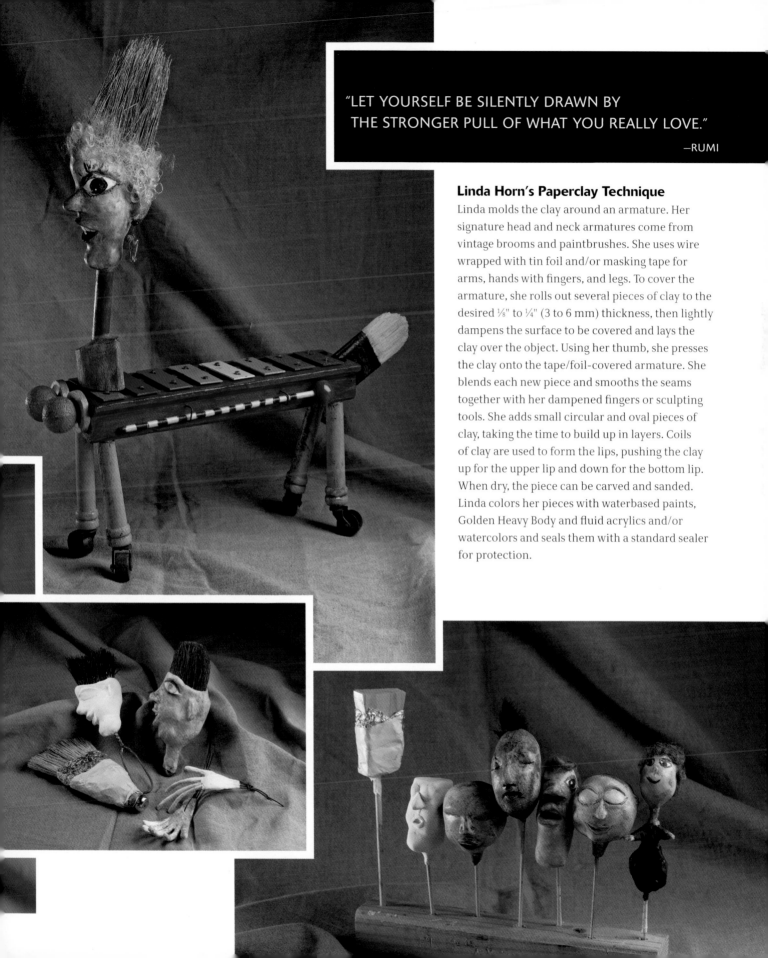

Linda Horn's Paperclay Technique

Linda molds the clay around an armature. Her signature head and neck armatures come from vintage brooms and paintbrushes. She uses wire wrapped with tin foil and/or masking tape for arms, hands with fingers, and legs. To cover the armature, she rolls out several pieces of clay to the desired ⅛" to ¼" (3 to 6 mm) thickness, then lightly dampens the surface to be covered and lays the clay over the object. Using her thumb, she presses the clay onto the tape/foil-covered armature. She blends each new piece and smooths the seams together with her dampened fingers or sculpting tools. She adds small circular and oval pieces of clay, taking the time to build up in layers. Coils of clay are used to form the lips, pushing the clay up for the upper lip and down for the bottom lip. When dry, the piece can be carved and sanded. Linda colors her pieces with waterbased paints, Golden Heavy Body and fluid acrylics and/or watercolors and seals them with a standard sealer for protection.

maggie Creshkoff

> *A doll is a miniature of our self; it serves as our proxy in a smaller world, a world that only seems playful. It carries for us forever—our hopes, our dreams, and our memories.*

About the Artist

Maggie Creshkoff is a potter who has worked solely with Cecil County clays since 1982. She lives with far too many cats, and has a wealth of usable materials at her fingertips, due to the pack-ratting instincts of her friends and family; in fact, she founded the Trashy Women in 2004 to better share the riches of a material world. Maggie is also a writer and a recorder player. Her current work explores the surprising beauty of decay, and shows the rich palette of natural oxidation contrasted with the colors revealed by the action of flame on clay. The juxtaposition of unexpected materials suggests figures seen at the edge of one's eye, while rusty angels and Madonnas, as formal as those seen in Byzantine and Flemish paintings, emerge from the neglected detritus of the workday world.

PROCESS Rusty Angel

This piece is in the authors' collection.

Maggie gifted me with this soulful rusty angel after Opie and I visited her and Bobby Hansson at their home affectionately called *"Maggie's Farm"* several years ago. Maggie's gentle and beautiful spirit is evident in her dolls, and her process is as simple as her dolls are powerful. She begins by letting metal rust for a number of years outside under wild cherry trees, and then presses local Maryland clay (high fire, iron rich from Stancills Sand and Gravel Inc.) into plaster molds made from doll faces. Once dry, she fires them in her kiln. She says she fires them where the flame actually goes, so they get *very* hot and many of them break. Once cool, she arranges and rearranges the pieces of metal and clay until it "feels" right and joins them with either E6000 glue or copper rivets.

Rusty Angel. According to Maggie Creshkoff, it's the local Maryland clay that contributes to the expressiveness of her kiln-fired faces.

bobby hansson

About the Artist

Bobby Hansson is the author of the wonderful book *The Fine Art of the Tin Can* (Sterling, 1999). He pioneered working with tin cans over forty years ago, and our first book was dedicated to him. He teaches creativity workshops, builds vehicles for kinetic sculpture races, constructs a variety of instruments from every imaginable material, and sends mail art to his friends that are works of art in and of themselves. He lives in Rising Sun, Maryland.

PROCESS   Harleykin

This piece was constructed from assorted tin cans and a simple wood shape for the torso, and Bobby's indelible style is so evident. All of his passions come into play here, as he's as comfortable with photography, tattooing, and metalsmithing as he is with transforming tin cans. Bobby began by nailing deconstructed tin to fit the wood torso he created. The arms and legs were formed from tin that had been cut into rectanglular shapes and rolled to form tubes. He added eyelets to the elbow and knee joints so that a wire could be inserted through the holes to connect the limbs. The upper arms were screwed into the wooden form and the feet were pop-riveted to the legs. Bobby created the face using a metalsmithing technique known as repoussé, which is similar to metal embossing in that it raises or pushes out a design in some areas of the metal—in this case the face. He completed the piece with a flattened baby cup for a helmet.

Harleykin. Bobby Hansson's masterful and creative use of tin cans has inspired metal artists everywhere.

"BE NICE, HAVE FUN AND DON'T KILL ANYBODY."

—BOBBY HANSSON

Lynne Sward

" A stick with beast fur, possibly wrapped with leaves, could've been the first doll or figurative sculpture given to a toddler for amusement and to neutralize endless crying. Throughout the ages, dolls ranged from the simplest to the more sophisticated/realistic sculptures, and were created from an eclectic array of media and techniques. I suspect that in early tribal cultures, as well as current ones, art in the form of a doll can be imbued with a special indefinable spirit or essence. "

About the Artist

Lynne was fortunate to have been born into a loving, eccentric, and artistic family. She says, "We are from where we've been, and my early experiences living at home definitely impacted me and helped form my future." For more than forty-five years Lynne has balanced being a wife, mom, and grandmother with teaching and a full-time art career. Her art reflects her many points of view, interests, and philosophies. Her audience is exposed to a world filled with abundant texture, explosive color, complex patterns, mystery, wry humor, and elements of the unexpected. After many years of creating two-dimensional fiber works, having her work published in many books and exhibiting internationally in museums and galleries, this well-respected artist decided to make mixed-media dolls and other totemic sculptures, in addition to limited-edition wearable art. Always looking to broaden her horizons, Lynne is currently constructing vessels, sacred objects, and handmade books, and exploring personal metaphors that allude to her eclectic personality and past experiences with threads and fabrics.

PROCESS Wisdom Spirit

Wood scraps, blocks, dowels, and bamboo offer many opportunities for creativity, especially when making one-of-a-kind figurative sculpture. Not only do they fulfill our "going green responsibilities," these materials are very inexpensive and can be used effectively in simple design forms. This piece evolved from unfinished pine wood that Lynne transformed into a mixed-media figure honoring Buddha. She sanded and gessoed the wood, added multiple layers of paint and paper, and added finishing touches of colored pencil scribbles. The basic structure for the legs is a ¼" (6 mm) dowel rod with papier-mâché padding. Lynne used the same size dowel rod to attach the head to the rectangular body. Lynne's technique for papier-mâché involves applying watered-down wallpaper border adhesive over torn strips of newspaper. She wrapped the legs with several layers of wet newspaper strips. When they were dry, she used acrylic paint to color the legs and added a final scribbling with colored pencils to blend with the look of the body. She made the book from different papers and Asian ephemera that she found at an Asian grocery store and the covers from mat board. Bamboo sticks from an extensive bamboo grove in her backyard were used to attach the front covers and pages to the back cover. Lynne glued and nailed the back cover of the finished book to the front of the wood substrate.

Wisdom Spirit. An old piece of pine was transformed into the doll's body by Lynne Sward with her expert use of paint, papers, and colored pencil.

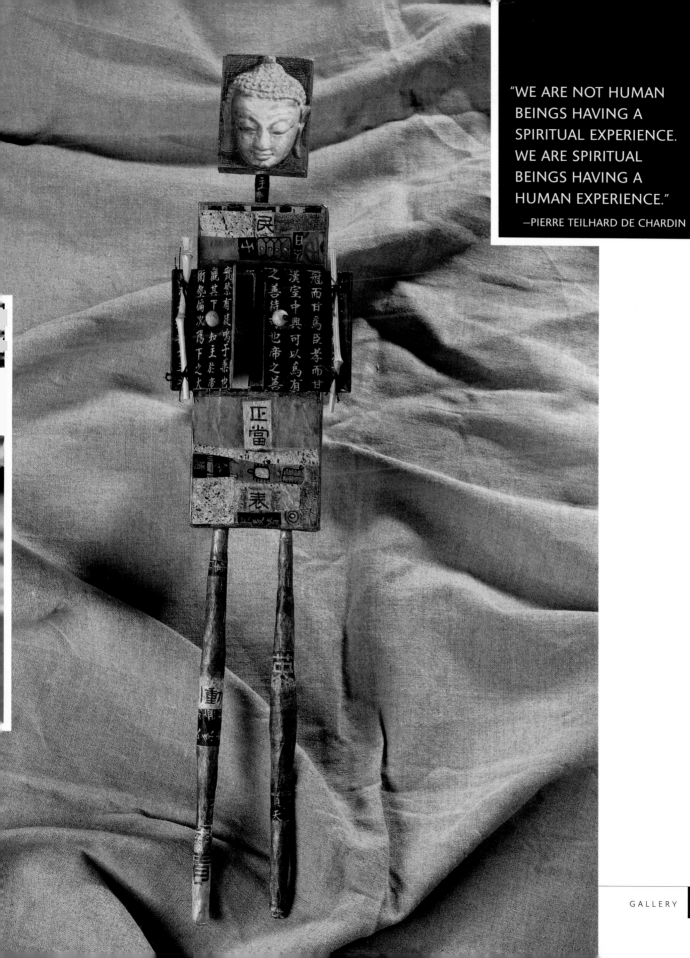

"WE ARE NOT HUMAN
BEINGS HAVING A
SPIRITUAL EXPERIENCE.
WE ARE SPIRITUAL
BEINGS HAVING A
HUMAN EXPERIENCE."
—PIERRE TEILHARD DE CHARDIN

pamela hastings

" Like the definition of art, a doll is a doll if I say it's a doll. It's usually humanoid and figurative. In some circles, I am known and taken seriously as a painter and sculptor, and I like to turn people's expectations upside down by calling my sculpture 'dolls.' My definition of dolls is definitely not your typical curly-haired, cute, dressed-in-ruffles miniature girls that people picture when I say I make dolls. I create my dolls with all the artistic skill with which I pursue any other art form. "

About the Artist

Pamela's work is constantly evolving and is a vital aspect of a life spent drawing and creating—a love affair with colors, images, fabrics, bits, and pieces. There is never an end to new combinations, new discoveries, and new layers of meanings. Her path is to work with art, words, women, and healing, while delighting in the creativity that we all possess and helping others discover their own gifts in the process.

PROCESS Chill

Pamela likes to collect stuff and even has friends who collect cool stuff for her. The body of *Chill* is the front of an old mailbox, a gift from a sculptor friend, and the head is clay, made in Central America. The base is a bunch of brass angles, also from a sculptor friend. Pamela said that she initially tried to construct the box part out of heavy-duty buckram covered by fabric, because sewing is the medium she's most comfortable with. Unfortunately it wasn't rigid enough to hold the weight of the door, so when we introduced her to Apoxie Sculpt, she was able to add enough stiff stuff to shore up the whole assemblage. Pamela likes to work with pieces that allow for an opening, so that other images can be placed inside and viewed from the outside. The title of the piece comes from a brass disc that fit perfectly into the indentation on the mailbox.

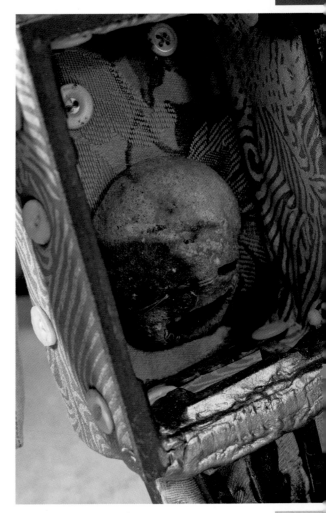

Chill. Pamela Hastings created a small assemblage inside the niche of the mailbox/body of her doll.

"1—SHOW UP,
2—PAY ATTENTION,
3—TELL THE TRUTH,
4—STAY OPEN TO
RESULTS."
—ZUNI LIFE PATH

CHILL
033

Susan lenart kazmer

About the Artist

Susan is one of the most creative people I've been privileged to know and with each year she somehow manages to surpass herself. Her work is drawn from her own life experiences and is about real life and real people. She is not afraid of experiencing all aspects of living, and portrays this through her work. She has always felt that the more you experience, the more layers of intricacy you are able to offer in your work. Susan was raised in Chicago, and during her teenage years, her upper middle-class family experienced financial crisis and was thrust into a life of poverty. With this hardship, she and her sisters gained a certain spiritual alliance and bond, and learned that positive things can result from poverty. Being very sensitive to her surroundings, a very young Susan couldn't help but notice the life around her—bars, drunks, pimps in full-length fur coats, and prostitutes. She saw it all and learned to use her own energies for protection, whether walking down the street in a deserted city neighborhood or during a stay in a four-star hotel, where social expectations were much different. Susan's work sustains her, as do the real people who surround her. Her self-published book, *Making Connections*, is a virtual feast about the art of cold-connections.

PROCESS The Opera Singer a.k.a. the Fat Lady

The idea of a Fat Lady in a circus side show is absolutely politically incorrect these days, but once upon a time when Susan was very young she attended a circus with her sisters. They went from room to room looking at all of the side shows. Some were so fake they were a complete disappointment, but the sisters were entranced by the Fat Lady who had her "show face" on and was reciting a disgusting script about a life of debauchery. Susan and her sisters innocently asked her how she could be up there on stage talking about herself. Suddenly her facial expression crumbled and she turned into a sensitive and real person. The hurt, hopelessness, and weariness in her eyes was overwhelming for Susan, and that vision has remained with her all of these years, inspiring her latest series of work called the Circus Troop.

The Fat Lady or *Opera Singer* is the first figure in this series; she sits in a frame and poses as a jewelry holder, carrying a collection of removable and wearable jewelry. Her adornment consists of four rings, a woven thumb ring, two pairs of hoop earrings, three fiber bangle bracelets, a stack of twelve sterling silver bangles and a "Letters to my Lover" charm bracelet as her skirt. The bracelet, which can actually be worn, is built from personal journal notes written by Susan to her husband, torn and rendered translucent, and applied to sterling silver organic, hand-hammered forms. She is a weary, but gaudy singer, worn down from life's performances, and is composed of a woven sterling silver cage with a music holder spine. Her arms lift up and down so the stack of bracelets can be removed. The entire piece is a play between fragility and strength. Her collection of four rings, worn as a hat, features the slush ring, which is a description of who she is and is composed of text-altered fiber, a cast silver component, and dictionary paper. Other components include cast objects, altered sterling silver wire, beads, sheet metal, resin, fiber, feathers, and paper, which are joined with a series of cold join attachments. Additional techniques that Susan used are simple soldering, casting, weaving, and stitching.

The Opera Singer. This charm bracelet, which forms the doll's tutu, was made using fragments of love letters that Susan Lenart Kazmer wrote to her husband.

jill marie shulse

"A doll is an object that can be admired when displayed, or lovingly handled and kept close to the heart. It can hold lots of memories from the past and provide a sense of security. It is something that can be loved, cherished, and held dear whether it is commercially manufactured, or handmade from the heart."

About the Artist

Creativity has always been one of Jill's passions, an escape where there are no rules and her imagination can run wild and take over as she lets the ideas she conjures up in her head become actual realities. As a self-taught artist, Jill enjoys working in a variety of mediums, but her main focus is found-object jewelry. Her art is a reflection of her personality, a glimpse into her soul, and a window into her thoughts. Bold, edgy, unusual, sometimes complex, other times simplistic, she almost always incorporates items of the past with items from the present. Her love of antiques, coupled with her own family history and old photographs, is thematic throughout her body of work.

PROCESS Treasure

Jill's very first workshop ever was with Opie and me several years ago at Valley Ridge in Wisconsin. The instant she walked through the door, I saw myself at her age—she was my *exact* mini-me. It gave me chills and we connected immediately and discovered we have at least a biz-illion things in common. We formed a strong bond that continually grows.

Jill's exquisite piece is wearable and began with the ring, which she constructed from precious metal clay. After firing it, she filled the bezel with text from an antique Bible. When the ring was finished, she immediately knew she wanted to somehow incorporate it into her doll for this book. Jill's doll body is composed of an antique Victorian cast-iron wall clip, a portion of an Eastlake thumb-latch plate, the tines of a silver serving fork, and a vintage brass rosette on which she created a bezel from sterling bezel wire. She placed a photograph of her great-grandmother inside the bezel, covered the image with a glass magnifying lens, and worked the bezel down tight over the lens to seal it. The entire piece is connected with extensive wire-wrapping techniques, using 16-, 18-, and 20-gauge steel wire. Jill connected a bolt to the bottom of the rosette, covering it with a piece of metal tubing, on which the ring can slide on or off the neck piece. Jill also finished the reverse side of the neck piece with more wire-wrapping. The bail is 16-gauge wire coiled through a slot in the latch plate. For the necklace chain, Jill covered steel wire with leather, added some sterling beads and forged the links of the chain and clasp, again using 16-gauge steel wire. She used an antique key for the clasp mechanism.

"THE SOUL WOULD HAVE NO RAINBOW IF THE EYES SHED NO TEARS."

—JOHN CHENEY

Treasure. Jill Shulse created the most amazing removable ring using precious metal clay and vintage text as the headdress for her piece.

lynn whipple

"I love dolls. I played with dolls, and in a way . . . I still do! Dolls are a representation of ourselves, a perfect foil for our imaginations; they are about storytelling. Who cannot see themselves holding two dolls, and hopping them toward each other deep in made-up conversation? Funny . . . yes, and so universal. In my world, it was Barbie! I loved her, and I loved her clothes. In my young mind, I was playing at being grown up. My next-door neighbor had a set of dolls from around the world, which were each dressed up in their native costumes. I was fascinated by those dolls, and I think they fostered my love of travel and my interest in other cultures."

About the Artist

Being an artist allows Lynn to engage in her favorite game— the search for interesting combinations and then fitting them together to tell a story. Using found objects, collage, sewing, drawing, photography, and painting, her joy is the discovery of something fresh and funny, while still touching on the poetic. Lynn's hope is to relish the tiny delights of being alive, and to communicate these simple satisfactions through her work.

PROCESS Camille

As with all of Lynn's pieces, this one started with the "hunt" and a visit to a great junkyard in Chattanooga called the Estate of Confusion. There, Lynn spied an old dusty box filled with melted glass and was told they were old bottles that had been in a fire. She thought they were great looking! Back in her studio, she noticed a particularly beautiful melted bottle that seemed to be the perfect form for a figure. Lynn wrapped it in red wire and was able to fashion some thin legs, and used small drilled stones for feet. The head and shoulders came from an old photo and some copper sheeting. Lynn likes the simple and fragile feeling of this doll. The finishing touches include red thread and cowrie shells.

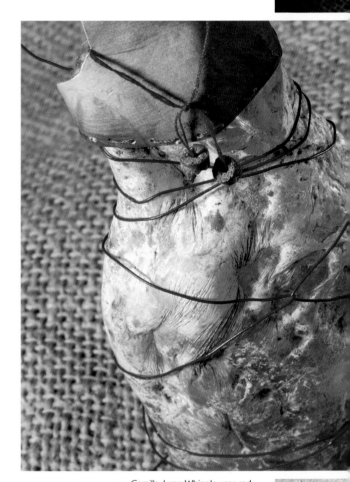

Camille. Lynn Whipple uses red thread and wire for attachment as well as embellishment.

john Whipple

"As a man, I think of a doll as a bit of nostalgia, a piece of youth. To me, this means it should look like it was heavily played with, and evoke a time when we gave names to our toys. To this day, I find I use materials that trigger the playfulness of my childhood."

About the Artist

John has been a working artist for more than twenty-five years. He currently creates his paintings and sculptures from McRae Studios in Winter Park, Florida. The studio was established by his family twenty years ago and currently provides studio space for twenty-four artists. Along with his artist wife, Lynn, their work is in numerous museum and city collections and can be seen in galleries, art festivals, books, and publications.

PROCESS Punch

John begins his work by rummaging through his odd collection of objects. He finds that being able to touch, examine, and make unusual combinations of pieces allows for a dialogue to ensue. His work moves through different stages of assembly until a story emerges. He knows that piece is complete when all the parts look like they were always together and that there is clarity in the story. John started this piece with a punching bag, which looked like a body. He tried a variety of heads on the body, heads that had been made for other sculptures and didn't work out. He likes to try a variety of heads to get a feeling of proportion. The head he chose was one that he had made while playing around with masking tape. The fur came from a "deconstructed" teddy bear, which he used to cover up the connection points and make the bear slippers. John thought the linear quality of the balloon was a good counterpoint to the weight of the punching bag, while enhancing the playfulness of the character.

Punch. This amazing head was made by John Whipple using masking tape.

judy wilkenfeld

> " A doll is a physical representation in the likeness of the chosen subject. "

About the Artist

Judy's "Visual Anthologies" tell the story of a life or lives, past or present. Presented in book form, wall art, or as an installation, Judy uses layering and the recontexturalization of materials to build the history of any subject matter. The mix of objects and style can certainly be termed *eclectic*; however, the pieces are always a reflection of a life. The realities of some life stories are often harsh, yet through her use of fabrics, textures, color, memorabilia, and/or found objects, Judy tries to remove some of the harshness without detracting from the essence of the piece. Blending the harsh with the soft, the simplistic with the highly detailed, and the static with the fluid, Judy presents a true reflection of the lives of those in the story she is telling. Her knowledge of customs, traditions and the spiritual nature of things, combines with her use of amended or new materials (made to look old), to represent the complexity of life's layers. Her pieces portray the emotions of life, and sometimes complex subject matters, such as the persecution of races, religions, and minority groups. To communicate the message of tolerance and understanding, through her art, is of utmost importance to Judy, in all her pieces.

PROCESS Parade

Almost all of Judy's art pieces involve some sort of research and this piece, which inspired her to research the Dada art movement, was no exception. In order for her to work her soul into this (or any) piece, Judy needs to find some relevance, hopefully personal. Almost immediately Judy found her link to Dadaism. Her piece pays homage to several interconnected images—to the performance in 1917 of the ballet "Parade" by Serge Diaghilev's Ballets Russes, to Tristan Tzara (founder of the Dada Movement), to Pablo Picasso and the other Dada artists who collaborated on the ballet, and finally to her grandfather, Jacob Simon Bloch, whose company made ballet shoes for the Ballets Russes. The ballet, considered a scandal at the time, had enormous influence and was hailed in its day as a perfect combination of dance, painting, sets, and music.

Judy's piece is set like a theater, and she chose to alter a doll form and dress it in the costume of the Conjurer, the Asian-inspired character in the ballet. As mentioned in the introduction, it has long been suggested that the word *dada* was chosen randomly from the Larousse encyclopedic dictionary, hence the addition of the Larousse dictionary within the piece. Coincidentially, six months prior to beginning this piece, Judy rescued twenty books and one of them was an original edition of the Larousse dictionary, which she uses in the piece, open so the word *Dada* is visible on the top right hand side of the page. Judy formed a shadowbox within the book with a replica of a Bloch ballet shoe, shellac (used by dancers on their toe shoes so they don't slip on stage), hessian (the core ingredient in the making of toe shoes), and Asian text. The Bloch Ballet Shoe company, now in its third generation, represents the connection between Judy, her family, the ballet, and Picasso—an important artist involved with the ballet and the Dada movement.

Parade. The Larousse dictionary that Judy rescued was destined for the dump.

Parade. An inside view of Judy Wilkenfeld's theater, complete with the knife pointing to the word *Dada*.

michael deMeng

" I think that a doll is more than a mere toy; it is something much more profound … it's an extension of the child's self. It is the child portraying itself in a fantasy world where it has control, since typically a child has little control in an adult world. And when "grown-ups" collect dolls … what is that? Perhaps it is also an extension of the self, but in this case it seems like it might be the nostalgia of being a child again. Ironic … yes indeed. "

About the Artist

Michael's work is about transformations of the common into the sacred. Discarded materials find new and unexpected uses in his work; they are reassembled and conjoined with unlikely components, a form of rebirth from the ashes into new life and new meaning. These assemblages are metaphors for the evolutions and revolutions of existence: from life to death to rebirth, from new to old to renewed, from construction to destruction to reconstruction. These forms are examinations of the world in perpetual flux, where meaning and function are ever-changing.

PROCESS Hin-dude

Michael's work always starts with parts and pieces—a pile of things laying about. Bit by bit things get assembled, usually with few preconceived notions. Objects gradually ebb and flow until they all start to jive. Then comes the glue, the nails, the screws, the duct tape, the plaster, the paints, and the "whatever it takes" to allow this creation to take shape. In a way, it's the idea of trying to find the sculpture in the marble; in Michael's case it's trying to find meaning in a big pile of things that don't typically go together.

A unique interpretation of an Eastern diety by artist Michael deMeng

Opie and I had been experimenting with Robert's faux bone for about a year, when one evening in late March of 2006, I apparently did the one thing one should never do with it, so I phoned him. The first thing he said to me was "you torched it, didn't you?" I had. As it turned out, our schedule allowed us to attend an upcoming workshop with him at Touchstone that summer; we refined our technique, shared stories about growing up in New York, marveled at what we had in common, and had a completely wonderful time. Robert tends to work in a narrative way. At times, an object will suggest the idea for a piece by what it references in its previous life. For instance, a button keeps an opening closed, a mirror reflects the world, or a compass shows the way. An object can carry with it a story, mystery, or comment. How did the bicycle reflector get broken? Who wore the medal with a green star on it and what was it for? Why was that typewriter left to rust? Most of the time, there is no hierarchy for Robert. Whether it's a ticket stub, a broken shard, or precious metal, it's the design that is important not the material. And if that piece of "stuff" makes a better design, then that's what gets used.

> " Dolls, for me, are always representations of people. Similar objects depicting animals and such, are toys. Dolls are also demanding. Unlike photos, paintings, or other images of humans, dolls occupy the same space I do and cannot be relegated to hanging on the wall as simple decoration. Even when dolls are placed in a case, they still occupy a place in my space, not an imagined or fictional space. Their silence can be deafening and their stare, like a dagger. "
>
> —Robert Dancik

PROCESS Something from Nothing

This piece is exactly *Something from Nothing*! It was an example Robert used to illustrate the pairing of faux bone, a user-friendly and extremely versatile material that can be cut, carved, sawn, sanded, filed, hammered, polished, drilled, stamped, riveted, inlayed, dyed, and more (see Resources, page 158) and papier-mâché. I thought it looked liked a torso, so I asked him if he would be interested in a collaboration, and I took it home. I created the head in layers using a crushed bottle cap, watch face, gem tintype, and scrap tin, which I riveted to a sawn, patinated, and tabbed copper substrate. I wired bisque arms to the torso and completed the piece by wire-wrapping tengura charms, which come from Nepal, are used in healing ceremonies, and are worn to ward off evil spirits and negativity, to form a skirt.

Something from Nothing. This started as a class example of Robert Dancik showing the pairing of papier-mâché with faux bone, but to me it was the body of a doll.

Linda's definition of a doll and artist statement are on page 151.

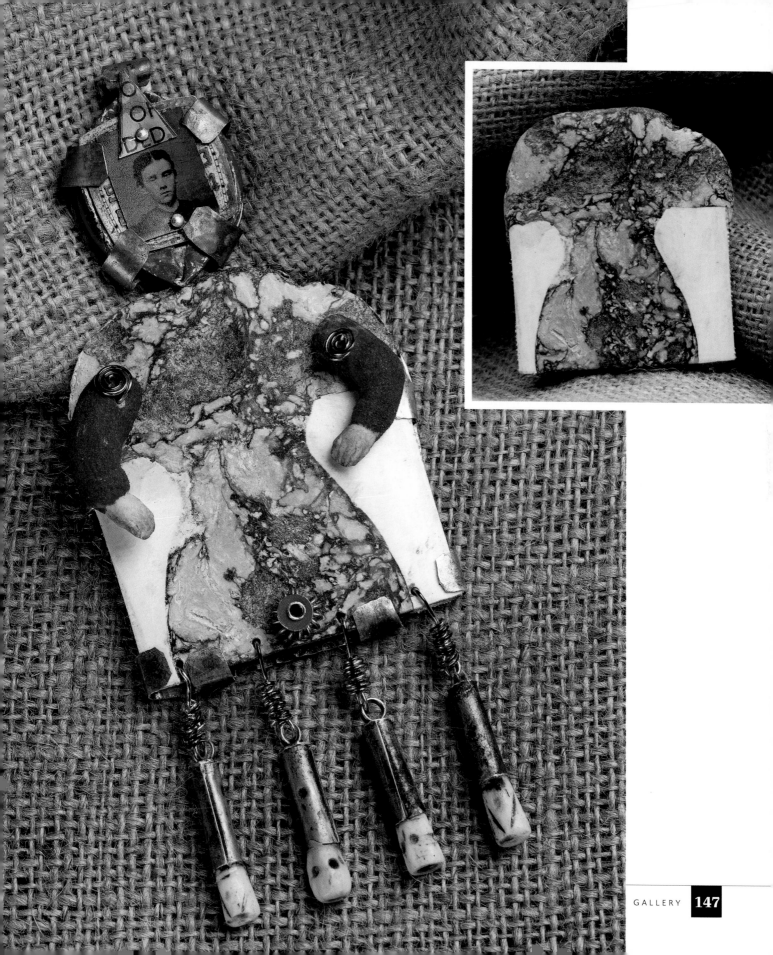

robert ebendorf

" The doll is an imaginary person that I might engage with verbally, in fantasy, or with tenderness. "

About the Artist

For the past twenty-five years, Robert Ebendorf has been re-employing existing materials by devising ingenious uses for objects that are underappreciated or overlooked by society to give them new life. By reassessing the meaning of artifacts of daily life, he often reverses the idea of what is precious. Robert is driven by a heartfelt passion to problem solve, create a narrative, a political comment, or just to make something beautiful. Many artists, including Opie and me, consider him an icon in the field of found-object art and have been inspired by him. His objects are not simply about refashioning the mundane; they reaffirm the value of that which otherwise might be without value.

PROCESS A Doll Asleep on a Broken Dish and The Doll That Went to Church

Ebendorf is known for working with unusual materials; those most often found in the alley, on the street, off the beach, or at the flea market. Objects such as fossils, animal claws, costume jewelry, medals, and coasters (as is evidenced in his pieces here), even pull tops from lids, have found their way into his art. And, it is exactly this sense of astonishment that gives his pieces their value. It is the profound incongruity between what they are made from, and what they are now, that so engages the imagination.

"I CAN'T UNDERSTAND WHY PEOPLE ARE AFRAID OF NEW IDEAS, I'M AFRAID OF THE OLD ONES."

—JOHN CAGE

The Doll That Went to Church. This broken and abandoned doll was given new life when Robert Ebendorf resurrected her ... so to speak!

A Doll Asleep on a Broken Dish. A few accessories and a jewel-encrusted aluminum coaster are the only things Ebendorf's doll needs to take a relaxing nap.

Opie o'brien

"Dolls are gifts to humanity. From the people who make them, to the children of all ages who embrace them, dolls are objects that stimulate an invisible personal story that only exists in the imagination of its handler. Growing up with a brother, dolls were gender selective and limited to G.I. Joe, soldiers, cowboys, and Indians. It wasn't until art school and numerous trips to the Metropolitan Museum of Art and the Museum of Natural History, that I discovered the vast and artistic wealth of dolls from other cultures and their diverse connection to religion and mythology. Through this discovery, a new world revealed itself to me, and I began to recognize that contemporary icons such as Barbie and Shirley Temple seemed almost superficial in comparison to so many other wonderful creations."

About the Artist

Opie's conceptual approach to creating art was first developed through music when he was very young. As with visual art, music is fundamentally a human emotional experience. At an early age, Opie started formal music instruction that was based on structure, discipline, and exactness, precepts now firmly rooted in his brain. He was once told that "music is mathematics" and has had many teachers throughout his life who have helped refine the subtle nuances and redefine the aesthetics of musicianship. A double Gemini, Opie is artist, musician, composer, and soulmate simultaneously. He's been in music groups such as Tommy James and the Shondells and The Raspberries and has played and recorded with music icons throughout his career. Today he divides his time between teaching workshops and creating in his art and recording studios. No matter what he's working on, he tries to let structure and discipline be the backdrop of the piece. For Opie, the true success of a piece happens when it affects someone on a purely emotional level, for then it has touched the soul. His ultimate goal is to seamlessly fuse his love of music with his love of art.

linda o'brien

"For me, dolls represent a personal journey that has come full circle. While they have always been in my life, their appearance and roles have changed and evolved with time, as have I. Over the years I've defined dolls as playthings, companions, confidantes, betrayers, guardians, healers, secret keepers, storytellers, whisperers, and today I call them *Dadas*, but they have always consistently been path markers, ever-present along my long bumpy road back to "me." Devastated by the death of my father at five and learning I was adopted just a few years later completely shattered me. Left with no sense of "self," I built a wall and retreated into my imaginary sanctuary called *Linda-Land* and disconnected. The dolls I had then, Tiny Tears, Betsy Wetsy, and my beloved German "Walking" doll were banished because I felt they somehow betrayed me. In hindsight, I suppose My Aunt Fran was the catalyst in my redefining the doll with the more unusual ones she sent me, which included dolls that were not quite dolls that seemed to possess an energy strong enough to penetrate that wall. These figures whispered "what ifs" to me which sparked my curiosity, ignited my creativity, and eventually guided my artistic path. Together we restored balance to my once fractured universe and over time and space they morphed into the "dolls" that Opie and I create today, which we refer to as Dada Dolls, a whimsical series that celebrates the unusual and the absurd."

Peoples Choice. Linda and Opie chose vintage tin clickers for the hands of this doll. The body is an old Brownie camera. Opie and Linda altered a doll's head, gave her vintage tin hands, miniature bowling pin legs, and tin embellishments, including a tobacco tag that reads *Peoples Choice.*

About the Artist

As a self-taught artist, I create my pieces from an intuitive feeling rather than from a learned technique. This allows me to make and break my own rules. My style is simple, understated, rather primitive, and never fully planned in advance, although in the end I do seem to eventually merge with my original concept, if only on an abstract level. My work, although very eclectic, consistently honors the feminine archetypes to which I feel a strong connection. The fact that I do this using organic, recycled, and found materials, just makes it all the better.

Man Boy. A piece of driftwood and other objects found on the lakeshore, plus an old harmonica, became the head of Opie and Linda's box-construction Dada.

The body is a box, purchased in Mexico, that was used as a measuring device for grain. Linda and Opie filled it with altered vintage printer's type. The head is a collection of found objects from the lake, and the mouth an old harmonica. One arm is a doll's arm, the other a part from a fishing reel. The legs are vintage blocks and they used tiny shoe lasts for the feet.

Lala Dada. Vintage tin and a children's block became the perfect body for this whimsical piece from Linda and Opie.

The body is a vintage children's block embellished with scrap tin and a bottle cap. A piece of scrap with the words *La La La La La* was how she got her name. Her head and arms are found objects from the lake and her eyes are old conus shells and glass heart beads. Vintage wood beads and miniature bowling pin legs complete the piece.

Lost in Translation. On this page, Opie and Linda pay homage to the Saturday market in Revel, France.

The body of this Dada is a vintage touring map that Linda and Opie heavily embellished and altered to pay homage to their month of teaching two workshops in the South of France. The doll's head was made from found materials, her hair is telephone and copper wire, and her arms and legs are recycled doll parts.

The Emperor's Scribe. An inside view of Opie and Linda's piece. More than 180 found objects were incorporated into this 4' (122 cm) Dada sculpture.

This piece was one of the finalist pieces that toured several United States contemporary art museums in a show called Transformation: Contemporary Works in Found Materials, the Elizabeth R Raphael Founder's Prize Exhibition. It's 4' (122 cm) tall and composed solely of recycled and found materials including a bicycle axle headdress, coffeepot head, bottle caps, and glass eyes in an optometrist test lens frame, saxophone and flute parts, a brass hose fitting for the mouth, typewriter keys, and tokens. The body is a wood assemblage made from a vintage artist paint box that houses a collection of vintage printer's type blocks, pen nibs, tins, a doll head, tobacco tag, and car emblem. That box sits inside a child's wood toy wagon that holds wood alphabet blocks. The front/door and sides are embellished with tin oil can and license plate parts, vintage pencils, Tinkertoys, and vintage camera parts. His "who-ha," a small aerosol can and silver salt and pepper shakers, makes him anatomically correct. The arms and legs are shed birch sticks with plumbing parts, electrical fuses, and springs. The legs are banded with inner-tube rubber, held with upholstery tacks, and set into a cinder block retrieved from the shores of Lake Erie.

The Emperor's Scribe. The head, created from a coffeepot, vintage optometrist equipment, a bicycle axle and more, are just a few of Opie and Linda's favorite things!

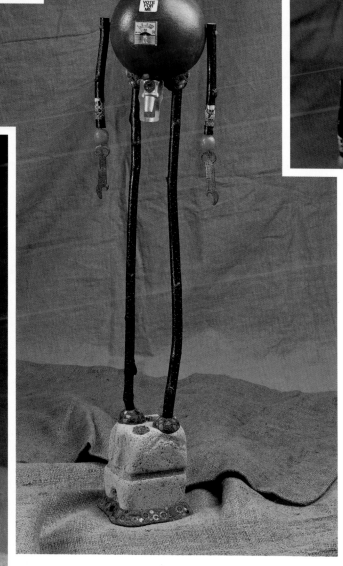

Which Way Is Up. Treasures from the lake and conus shell eyes are some of the objects Opie and Linda used to create this recyclabot's head.

The body is a hard-shell Lagenaria gourd and one of the many pieces in Linda and Opie's ongoing Recyclabot series. Everything else is repurposed or found materials with shed birch arms and legs. The piece stands about 2' (61 cm) tall.

Fashionista. Opie and Linda made this Dada using various children's blocks, bone, tin scraps, and hangers. Her face is etched nickel and she sports a very fashionable Christmas bulb headpiece.

The body, head, and base substrates are vintage children's blocks and Tinkertoys. The face is etched, the actual body is bone, her supports are metal hangers, and the embellishments are tin fragments and a Christmas tree light bulb.

artist contact information

Michelle Allen
www.allendesignsstudio.com
www.allendesigns.typepad.com

Brian Andreas
www.storypeople.com

Michelle Renee Bernard
www.yesterdaystrashart.com
www.michellereneebernard.blogspot.com
michelle@yesterdaystrashart.com

Clarissa Callesen
www.clarissacallesen.com
www.clarissacallesen.blogspot.com
clarissacallesen@gmail.com

Wendy Casperson
wenjunn@comcast.net

Lynda Crawford-Sheppard
lmcrawford63@hotmail.com

Maggie Creshkoff
www.backlogpottery.com

Robert Dancik
www.robertdancik.com
playcik@yahoo.com

Michael deMeng
www.michaeldemeng.com
www.michaeldemeng.blogspot.com
assemblage@michaeldemeng.com

Linda Drake
linda@lunar-designs.com

Joyce Durand
www.durandart.com
craftie.joy@gmail.com

Robert Ebendorf

Shain Erin
www.shainerin.com

Bobby Hansson
bobbyhansson@gmail.com

Pamela Hastings
www.pamelahastings.com
pamela@pamelahastings.com

Linda Lou Horn
lindalouhorn@yahoo.com

Judith Hoyt
www.judithhoyt.net
judithhoyt@earthlink.net

Susan Lenart Kazmer
www.susanlenartkazmer.net
susanlenartkazmer@roadrunner.com

Chelsey Kohler
www.w0rkinpr0gress.wordpress.com

Diane Kurzyna a.k.a. Ruby Re-Usable
www.rubyreusable.com
www.rubyreusable.com/artblog
rubyreusable@gmail.com

Jane Leppin
peacockstale@gmail.com

Leighanna K. Light
www.lklight.blogspot.com
lklight@copper.net

Keith Lo Bue
www.lobue-art.com
keith@lobue-art.com

Eric Allen Montgomery
memoryboxer@yahoo.ca

Linda O'Brien
www.burntofferings.com
www.burntofferings.typepad.com
gourdart@burntofferings.com

Opie O'Brien
www.burntofferings.com
www.burntofferings.typepad.com
gourdart@burntofferings.com

Lauren Ohlgren
www.sheproject.com
lauren@ohlgren.com

Lynne Perrella
www.lkperrella.com

Suzanne Sattler
suesattler55@yahoo.com

Shelley D. Schorsch
sschorsch@mac.com

Janette Schuster
www.visualapothecary.com

Jill Marie Shulse
www.jillmarieshulse.blogspot.com
jillstng@wi.rr.com

William Skrips
www.wmskrips.com
handmade@netcarrier.com

Lynne Sward
610arts38@cox.net

Terry Taylor

Deb Trotter
www.cowboyssweetheart.net
cowboyssweetheart.typepad.com
debtrotter1@gmail.com

Gail Trunick
www.gailtrunick.com
trunickstudio@earthlink.net

Lynn Whipple
www.whippleart.com
jxlwhipple@aol.com

John Whipple
www.whippleart.com
jxlwhipple@aol.com

Judy Wilkenfeld
www.visualanthologies.blogspot.com
www.redvelvetcreations.blogspot.com
judy@redvelvet.net.au

resources

Aves Apoxie Sculpt, synthetic self-hardening clays and mâché products
www.avesstudio.com

Brass Fasteners and Washers
www.office-supplies.us.com

Cold Rolled Steel
G-T Stained Glass and Tin Works
505.247.9322 (no website) Albuquerque, New Mexico, or online

Eyelets, Brads, Tape, and Embellishments
www.coffeebreakdesign.com

Faux Bone
www.fauxbone.com

Golden Paint, Fluid Acrylics, Various Mediums, GACS, Gesso, Molding Paste
www.goldenpaints.com, craft and art supply stores, and online

Heat-Set Metallic Foils
www.dickblick.com and online

Mini- and Micro-Fasteners and Nut Drivers
www.micromark.com
www.reactivemetals.com
www.microfasteners.com

Objects and Elements Jewelry Supply
www.objectsandelements.com

Paper Perfect and Paper Perfect Accents from DecoArt
www.decoart.com

Polymer Clays, Paperclay, Rubber Stamps, Stencils, Brushes, Crayons, Flexible Molds and Molding Kits, Rigid Wrap, Acrylic Paints, Mediums and Glues, Inclusions for Making Handmade Paper
Most craft stores and online

Quilter's mini iron, grommets, pattern tissue, cheesecloth, Lutradur
www.joann.com and online

Ranger Ink, distress and various inks, crackle paints, craft sheets
www.rangerink.com, craft stores, and online

Tin Cans
www.eBay.com, yard and garage sales, flea markets, and secondhand stores

Tools, unmounted rubber stamps and more
www.burntofferings.com

Wire, nails, screws, screw Eyes, fasteners, screen. heavy-duty tin snips, pop rivet gun and rivets, sandpapers
Hardware and home improvement stores

about the authors

Opie O'Brien distinguished himself at an early age when his Bumble Bees were voted best in third grade and hung on the bulletin board outside the principal's office at PS 33 for a month.

Linda O'Brien doesn't remember third grade.

Encouraged by his early success, Opie took music lessons, studied art for three years at SVA and honed his craft. He joined the Raspberries after their third album, played Carnegie Hall at age twenty-four and Madison Square Garden at twenty-nine. He's played with major bands and music legends. Discipline was his middle name.

Linda, being adopted, never knew her middle name, assumed Peter Pan was her biological father, and became a free-spirited self-taught artist, workshop instructor, and writer. When their paths crossed (collided) in 1984, they discovered they were opposite sides of the same coin . . . soulmates!

While their individual styles complemented each other, as a team they truly excelled, and Burnt Offerings Studio is the result of their combined efforts.

New York City transplants, they are full-time artists living on Lake Erie in Ohio with their cat Angelus and his cat Angel. They teach art workshops nationally and internationally based on several of the techniques in their book *Metal Craft Discovery Workshop* (North Light, 2005) and their Who's Your Dada: Redefining the Doll Series, which this book is based on. They appreciate the unusual and collect everything from space toys to burial dolls. These themes influence their work, which has been featured in more than twenty-seven books, several magazines, galleries, solo and group shows, museum gift shops, CD, TV, and private collections.

acknowledgments

This book began as a vision, that grew into an idea, and reached fruition, as a result of the talented artists, both professional and students, who graciously accepted our invitation to define a doll and share their processes with you. Your generosity was limitless and we thank each of you. Without you this particular book would never have been written.

To Mary Ann Hall, our editor and now friend, who believed in our vision for this book from the very beginning, and pushed us beyond our technological comfort zone, for which we are so grateful.

To Winnie Prentiss, the art department, and our new "family" at Quarry Books, who saw early on that this book was more than the sum of its parts. We thank you for all of your support.

To Dina Rossi, our more than friend and photographer extraordinaire, who continues to capture our best side. This wouldn't be fun without you and we look forward to the next fourteen years of long studio shoots, great music, irreverent humor, and pima quotes.

To our family and friends who enrich us, and our four-legged children, Angelus and Angel, who fill our days and nights with laughter.

And to my Aunt Fran . . . who continues to watch over me.

"WE ARE CARETAKERS OF THE MUNDANE AND THE ORDINARY. WE WORK WITH ORGANIC, RECYCLED, AND FOUND MATERIALS, BECAUSE THEY SEEM TO HAVE A VOICE THAT MUST BE HEARD, A STORY THAT MUST BE TOLD, AND A LIFE THAT WOULD OTHERWISE BE TOO SOON FORGOTTEN."

MISSION STATEMENT